A decade ago we lost a great writer but above all a great friend.

A Space to Write is dedicated to Nick Darke.

29th August 1948 – 10th June 2005.

Photographer – Steve Tanner

Interviews – Amanda Harris

Editor – Emma Mansfield

Artwork – Paul Colledge, Revival Design

Production – TJ International, Cornwall

A SPACE TO WRITE
First edition published by KEAP, Cornwall, 2015.
Copyright Steve Tanner & KEAP 2015.

ISBN 978-0-9933958-0-2
www.keap.org.uk T: 07712 331421 E: amanda.harris@keap.org.uk

A SPACE TO WRITE

'Every writer faces the blank page or blank screen and simply has to make a start. It is a great encouragement to us all, that the great writers have all had to begin like this'

Foreword by Michael Morpurgo

Each of us has to find a way to begin writing. I have my way, not the best way - there is no best way - but my way. I think every writer has to read widely, to live a life as interesting and involved as possible, to meet people, go places, to keep eyes and ears and heart open. We have to drink the world in, know it, develop our concerns, and so discover what it is we care about.

That said, I spend weeks, months, years sometimes, in what I call my 'dreamtime', a period during which I settle on my choice for the seed corn of my story, a story I care about, that I want to write, need to write. I do not begin until I am ready, till the story is ready to tell, not formed entirely, but I know the world I am writing about, from memory, from research, and I know the people in my story, know them so well I want to tell their story.

When I write, I try to forget that I am writing at all. I simply tell it down onto the page, speak it down, warts and all. Then I read it out aloud, and rewrite and rewrite until I am happy with it. I write by hand, because I am used to doing it that way, so all this rewriting is done by hand too. Then I pass it on to someone who knows technology well, who produces a clean script, which I then tweak into a final version.

And where do I do all this? Long ago, as a young writer, I used to sit at a desk and write. Then I had trouble with my wrist and shoulder and back, and it became too painful to go on that way. I tried standing up at an easel and writing that way, but then my feet hurt! The solution came from a book I was reading, a biography of my writing hero, Robert Louis Stevenson. There was a photograph in the book on Stevenson of the great man, sitting propped up by pillows on his bed, his knees drawn up, writing away on a notebook. He looked relaxed, at complete ease, his back and shoulders supported. I tried it, it worked, and has worked now for years. So now I can say I write like Robert Louis Stevenson! Well, sort of!

Introduction

In the spirit of many of the writers in this book, I have put on my walking boots and set off down the lanes to think through writing this introduction. It's not a long walk but it is one I know well and have tramped for many years around Laity Moo (the 'r' is permanently erased from the signpost). I like it to be brisk but it also gives me time to read the hedgerows. It is currently early Autumn and the sycamore leaves are curling and black spotted, the cow parsley, exuberant in Spring, is now desiccated and skeletal, nettles bent heavy with seed are ensuring their survival and burrowed in the brambles' lair, the gift of blackberries. They are very Cornish hedges. And this book which began as a simple exploration of where writers choose to write has become a book about Cornwall and how Cornwall gives them the tools, the spaces, the inspiration (even if they are writing about events and places far away) to do so. How different would their work be if they lived in Norfolk or Shropshire?

The book is also propelled by working with young people on creative writing projects and wondering whether talking to the professionals could support work in education. How many writers choose to write in a room with thirty people gathered around a table? Out of this developed the idea for A Space to Write – the book and also a linked education project.

We teamed up with photographer Steve Tanner who is well known for his pictures of theatre and dance productions and for brilliantly capturing a fleeting moment. He photographed details of the writing space and the writers in conversation. He was exploring how to interpret the writer, their writing and their space. There is huge diversity in approach, with some writers needing total seclusion and silence while others seek out places where the hubbub of daily life is going on around them. For all, the physical act of writing is only part of the process and for the trying out of ideas, dialogue or rhythm many writers take to the cliff or footpaths, go cycling or jump on the train.

All the writers are linked to Cornwall either through being brought up here and/or living and working here now. It is a snapshot in time and we know there are many writers that we haven't been able to include – maybe there will be an opportunity for Space to Write Book 2? We have limited the book to 26 writers linked to the limited palate of 26 letters that a writer uses but from which every writer builds a distinct and individual voice. The book is bookended by illuminating writing by Michael Morpurgo and the late Nick Darke on their way of writing. And looking to the future there is a section on very young writers who are inspired to write and already have a passion for stories.

We are very grateful for the generosity of the writers giving us access to their private dens and for donating an excerpt of their work to the book It has been an adventure criss-crossing Kernow in Steve's van to be welcomed by coffee, cake and stories. We hope the reader will have as much fun with this as we have had in creating it.

Proceeds from this book will support writers working in schools through our programme of the same name, A Space to Write.

Amanda Harris

Ponsanooth 2015

WRITERS IN CONVERSATION

Bert Biscoe

Megan Chapman

Jon Cleave

Jane Darke

Bob Devereux

Mac Dunlop

Patrick Gale

Rebecca Gregson

Carl Grose

Alyson Hallett

Seth Hampshire

Pol Hodge

Mark Jenkin

Mercedes Kemp

Liz Kessler

Philip Marsden

Callum Mitchell

Graham Mitchell

Annamaria Murphy

Simon Parker

Jane Pugh

Bill Scott

Pauline Sheppard

Penelope Shuttle

D M Thomas

Elaine Ruth White

Bert Biscoe

Politician, Poet, Performer
Truro

Every day for the last five years I've written a poem a day. Once completed they are printed off and placed in a plastic folder for that month and then transferred to a lever arch file on a shelf in my room. Each month can have a different theme, voice or can change tack. But they all reflect the 'now'. I am influenced by the beat poet Charles Bukowksi who wrote very quickly about 'the now'. Harold Nicholson's Diaries chronicled the period he was involved in politics for over thirty years. These poems may serve a similar function.

When writing poetry I write quickly, work at it, chop bits out … you have to be tough to make the poem work, the internal rhythm. I like playing with internal rhymes. Rhythm is more important to me than structure – I can do a quatrain but would rather play with internal rhythm.

For me it is the importance of capturing the moment – a Cornish lane, high hedges, trees overhanging, enclosed, winding, come upon a gate, carry on, turn back – that is the moment you are seeking.

I never re-read a poem.

This space is the only one I've got. There are thousands of books and I know exactly where everything is – it is well insulated. I do keep objects but not as inspiration. I must have a keyboard.

Poetry is my procrastination from doing other things. As a Cornwall Council cabinet member I get 150 emails a day… each one a poem in itself!!

Of Time's Massage

Early mornings discreetly clank
Pints and empties – Milko and Me
Struggle to retain his music,
Percussive treble of bygone,
In the mix – once a year or so,
I beside road, Green Man pressed,
Spinal curl of lumbar tailback,
Choked distributor road, choked town –

Poor dirty old civis – plastic signage,
Plastic windows, 'shops don't open
Till ten these days!': 'Poor old place!' –
Sits forward and fails to raise
A hand to muffle and catch its cough –

There are books and cards
And nowadays a website,
Urbane crocodiles dab kerchiefs
To eye-corners moistened,
Yet careful not to smudge
Mrs New Labour Leader's Latin –
Americano mascara, it will not do
For a branded town to weep
On weekdays, and so, early morning,
A brisk chamois of pigeon
Leathers the sky, turns to dance
In formation its sunrise ballet –

Pink clouds bely the de-flocked shepherd
Whose warnings cry between pages
Of history and reminiscence, each
Uncertain of the other's provenance,
And each, gathered in sets to shelve
The masquerade of learning
Through breakfast and early morning
Cups of tea, routine begs indulgence,
Sinews loosen, thought wanders –

As I walked home last night
From General Purposes in its hallowed room,
Watercolours and oils obdurate in witness
Of business, sewers and CCTV – 'It's you and me'
Old Arnold's voice intones from Kenwyn's
Yew and garlic fields. 'We must think
What's underneath and above,
How it works, the machinery of town –
Somebody needs to know where to dig
A hole when the phones go down!'

The early morning house is noisy
In its flush, taps run for good water,
Boiler fired and metal's soul expanded –

As I walked home two gulls
Shrieked from the lawyer's roof,
A solstice tide sat risen and thick
With down-washed soil from harvest
Rendered fields – hot jazz flew
From the Frenchman's empty
And stylish Monday evening bar:
Two gulls preached, their rhetoric
Stripped time and tale from the bridge,
The street lay, littered, naked,
Not a heel clicked nor wagtail flicked –

I sensed myself a lone congregant,
Only embarrassment held me back
From taking-a-knee – their word,
Whatever sense it made, held me –

The Green Man flashed and bleeped,
Urgent to usher me over, safe passage
Of helpless being to safe haven
And retirement's lost and broody
Greeting. I gathered the town together
To carry on camomile expeditions
Through continents of Jung, and woke –

A Daddy Long Legs trapped,
I use a bread knife to prise it from
The bars of window's sash to morning air –

A shepherd dashes parting daubs
Of rouge to September clouds – pigeons
Map their Fancier's journey
Across a dawn-scrapped poem cast
Aside, re-made and filed – I turn
To run the tap, to kettle, to cup,
To run a cup upstairs in mimicry
Of routine and rhythm – of Time's massage.

Megan Chapman

Performance Word Artist and Youth Worker
Penryn

For me it's not about the space, it's about what you bring to it. As long as it is quiet enough, or no conversation directed at me, I will write directly on to the laptop. Trains and flights are good where I can't do anything else and can get into the zone to write in my head. It's the reaction to people that creates stories so I wouldn't go to a coffee shop to write.

I can be pondering an idea, then get into the flow and then I write. I don't make myself do it; rather I'm drawn to it. It might only be a couple of days a month so I don't put pressure on myself to write and I don't do it unless I want to.

I have a passion for rhymes and metaphors and writing that identifies with people across class and backgrounds. I want my work to relate to people and give people a voice. I was originally inspired by Eminem and, like him, my aim is to always write clearly and honestly, hoping to reach rather than exclude people.

I like to see people through their eyes, to give voice to someone who doesn't have one. I like political topics on the edge of things, the unsaid, the stories that could be missed. Situations in life need a different voice. I draw on my own experiences but also interpret others' and make it accessible – so giving as many people as possible the chance to relate to writing. All my work is delivered to be read out loud. I started out as a rap artist and have gradually moved into spoken word and see myself as a performance word artist, a new title.

When I've finished a piece of writing I get someone to edit it for me – I hate doing it! I'm dyslexic so I don't find it easy. But I do find it easy to perform and write. I love the 'concentrated squash' – telling a story in three and a half minutes creates a clever flow, using every part of the verse to create impact. The best piece I've done was written in fifteen to twenty minutes. I have a voice in my head – a judgemental, negative one. I have to turn it off, accept it, then it goes away. So there are two voices in performance.

I work out the rhythm and rhyme in my head but they are tweaked on paper.

I'm interested in people and emotions, social stuff but not objects. My laptop is useful but I am not sentimental about it. I can work in any chair – I don't even need a table.

I don't really procrastinate as I write when I want to. It's a real passion for me. I would love writing to be my full time job and maybe one day it will be, but for now I'm happy doing what I love when I can. This is such a good time for the spoken word and my busiest year to date.

See Your by MCMC

See the pain pinned up on your face
See the difference that you make
See you listen and you wait
See what someone already take
See the snake wrapped round your neck
See the tape draped round the deck
See the dead body you won't forget
See those eyes you never met
See that lost soul you project
See your tossed body you forget
See a version of your person
See your deserving tried still learning
See the unearthing and talking
See the disturbing paths you're walking
See your story through your lens
See the gory see your trends
See your confidential see potential
See your benchmark 'n strong heart
See you embark in a dark path
See your path was never lit
See a candle born with no wick

See the cover mothered in pain
See the uncovered wearing their parent's shame
See a spinning weather vane?
See your sinning is your claim
See you're caught up in a web
See your self taught head
See your dread and your fear
See your tears as I hear
See your life see your day
See your kite please fly today

Jon Cleave

Writer, Singer, Illustrator, Performer
Port Isaac

I have my own room where I can shut all the doors – Caroline thinks I'm an anti-social bugger, but I need it to be silent to write. And it can't be cold or draughty, and I need my nice big window to look out at all the birds on the feeder outside (a nice posse of long-tailed tits is my favourite), and of course I must have loads of mugs of builder's tea. It's all a bit diva-ish, isn't it?

I didn't choose this space; it's our old living room, and I'm really fortunate that it's evolved into mine over the years. There's a few special objects dotted around: in particular an old plaster apple that my Nan used to keep in her fruit bowl in the front room of her house in Padstow, and a Staffordshire flat back ornament of Dick Turpin and Black Bess from Aunt Sue's Port Isaac cottage. She used to keep it in her 'best' cupboard. They're just things that have always been around. Then there's a small clay figure I made in art class, of a bald middle-aged man sporting a jaunty, walrus moustache; that's a bit scary…

I've written the seven Gully books in here, and Nasty Pasty and lots of songs. Sometimes I'll write longhand into a bound workbook on the kitchen table; if I ever remembered to buy a bottle of ink I'd love to write using a proper pen like I used to at Bodmin Grammar. We weren't allowed to use Biros. Standards, you see!

I wrote the first page of Nasty Pasty, virtually as it's been published, on a beach in Kefalonia. We're off with the same friends to Croatia this year, so I'm expecting great things for the sequel. Once I've got a start, I like to plot things out on a flowchart on A3 sheets, with all the plots and subplots interweaving. Then I feel safe to start writing, and things seem to evolve out of the structure. I hate leaving any elements untied.

If I'm illustrating the Gully books, I don't need silence, I spread everything out on the kitchen table and whack on the Earth, Wind and Fire and Doobie Brothers and Barry White, and then splash the paint around in full groove to sad ole Dad's seventies disco kitchen collection. It's quite a sight.

If I can drag myself out of bed, the mornings are very definitely the best writing time, really rich from six to ten. After that, I tend to get caught up in all the real life stuff going on around me!

From Nasty Pasty, Published by Jon Cleave 2014

Digory Hicks was moving forward as founder and proprietor of the lonelyfarmersheartsclub.com, a sort of bucolic online knocking shop for those ruddy-faced, soil-toiling sons of Kernow who found mainstream socialising just too much of a challenge.

He checked his website and answered the various queries of his clientele who were generally, but not exclusively, of the agricultured persuasion. There were wind and sun farmers, wave and tide farmers, grant and granny and granfer farmers. There were organic farmers, arable farmers and 'orrible farmers, just a very few gentleman farmers, and quite a lot more beastly, filthy old farmers, invariably clad in threadbare corduroy trousers held up precariously with orange bailer twine.

Except, of course, when reposed in lay-bys.

Jane Darke

Writer, Artist, Filmmaker, Polymath
Porthcothan

I like writing on the move, trains are good, distance from home is helpful but not essential. Walking on beaches helps to clear my head but I also work beaches for finds so it's part of my schedule. I like to sit at my bedroom window which overlooks the bay to read.

This room is a good space as I have all my projects to hand. Sometimes I write in bed, in the winter, when the house is cold! I wrote the early stages of Held by the Sea in bed, completely relaxed I let my mind wander. I guess that's why trains are good too, I know that there's nothing else to do on the journey so I relax. In recent years I've been to New Zealand, Africa, the West Bank, I can write anywhere. I keep a notebook for drawings and writing and I take photographs. I like a fast flowing felt tip pen to get thoughts down and then edit on the computer in this room. I have no routine; I write when I want, sometimes all night. Writing is less demanding than painting and drawing which require more physical engagement. I don't like to edit my paintings, they need to be right first time, which requires immediate, full concentration in short bursts. Whereas I can drift into writing then suddenly realise that I've been working for four hours without a break. I am driven by deadlines – whichever project has the nearest deadline gets done first. Film making is another sort of discipline. I spend more time with people, interviewing or editing, which is good for me. I love film editing, bringing everything together, and I love going out with my camera, getting absorbed in a subject. Everything feeds everything else.

All the objects in this room have significance. I write on my mother's table, that vase she used for the first daffodils each year, that box holds Nick's (Nick Darke, the playwright) father's sextant. The drawers are full of our beachcombing collection – sea beans, lobster tags, bird skulls, lighters from all over the world. There are Nick's fishing diaries and his father's from the farm, as well as one of each of Nick's manuscripts.

I often have people visit the house, including schools. Children and students watch The Wrecking Season before they come. I show them objects from the sea and tell their stories, it's become a performance, and then we go down on the beach to explore. We all have a really good time.

I also run The Nick Darke Award with Falmouth University, £6,000 for a writer, and I curate St Eval Archive, a wonderful collection of photographs and recorded memories.

Do I procrastinate? Not really. The good thing about being a polymath is that I move from one project or art form to another and my work is so much part of my daily life that everything is relevant. I'm always producing something, in fact I have a problem with wasting time. My grandfather was a Methodist minister so it probably stems from that, maybe it got worse when my partner died. I am aware that time is precious. The internet is a distraction!

From Held by The Sea by Jane Darke

Published by Souvenir Press, 2011.

David Nash makes monumental sculptures with raw wood from fallen trees. He cut a wooden boulder and followed its course on film, in words, photographs and drawings, for twenty-five years as it was taken by melt water down a mountain to the sea.

If I found his wooden ball I'd roll it home.

What will I paint, or make?

My wreck collection is my inspiration, it expresses many things about the lives we lead. Raw plastic washes off our roads and follows water out to sea, on its way absorbing toxins we've made and can't control. Little balls of toxic plastic poison fish. Red plastic is fed by seabirds to their chicks. When we've used up all the oil we will all gather up the broken remains of plastic objects from landfill and the sea, as they already do in slums in India. We ship our rubbish to them, the remains of a precious resource squandered. This detritus defines us.

Peter Lanyon, a great Abstract Expressionist and Cornishman, glided to his death when drifting over fields and valleys for aerial views which inspired his work.

Alfred Wallis, a mariner, worked boats between Penzance and Newfoundland, he painted what he knew, paintings like maps or plans of harbours and boats, painted on anything.

Flattening the landscape is a good way to capture the relationship between land and sea. The horizon, division between the planet surface and its atmosphere, then disappears.

L.S. Lowry painted industrial landscapes in the North of England filled with people. He visited Cornwall and painted here. He painted a sea that could be anywhere, no land or boats or people, a grey sea meeting a grey sky at a faint line. The horizon is endless space represented by a single, unreachable, line. One way to paint it is to forget everything else so the line becomes profound, like a painting by Mark Rothko.

When the tide is very high, only a few yards from the gate, I don't need a towel. The bank is steep and the waves slam in at the last minute, they pile up and swirl across. I have strong legs so I stand firm as they hit, like Colossus. I take it steady and hold on until there's a little calm, then swim into the waves, go with it, pull as required by the force of water.

I get out beyond the surf to float on my back, facing the setting sun, like a cork. My feet rise up in front as a wave rolls under me.

Seals do this too, the grey seal, the most common here. They twist and turn through kelp, through gullies, between the islands and into sea caves, picking off crabs and lobsters as they go. I think they wait above my pots and take the lobsters. Sometimes one is there, head and shoulders out of water, as I pull up the empty pot. I talk to them but their black eyes don't give anything away.

 The pups are weaned at about three weeks, at six weeks they have their adult fur. As winter sets in many starve or die of exhaustion. They come ashore to rest. Leave them alone and keep your dog away, the beach is theirs not ours.

Sometimes a seal sees a wall of net with fish caught in it, they only eat the heads, the best bit. Fishermen shoot them. I've measured seal bodies decomposing on the beaches, a record for the Wildlife Trust. There aren't many fish in the sea and when all the fish are gone and we can't grow food because the climate's changed, we will eat the seal.

I brought some wood back from Rowan Cove, towed it behind the boat. As I entered the bay a seal came alongside and followed me in, flopped up onto the beach next to the boat,

'OK what now?'

It's rare to meet a wild animal, face to face, which has so little fear.

Bob Devereux

Poet, Librettist And Painter
St Erth

I see myself as a space organiser, but I have never quite managed to create a dedicated space for writing. I do have a new studio at the end of the garden and when it is fitted out I will certainly write there.

For the time being the whole house is my space. Where I decide to work varies with the situation and what feels right. Crucially I do need reference – I have a great many books which I regard as old friends, also a lot of paintings. My sitting room is wallpapered with OS maps which all resonate with meaning.

For me poetry is word music. I sound the words in my head when I am composing and only consign them to paper when a piece is near completion. When performing I seldom read my poetry from the page, but I do make an effort to learn the words; I know them.

When I am working, if I am alone, I often speak my words out loud, particularly if I am walking. Especially between the house and the train station. The rhythm of walking adds something to the creative process. I also find that it often speeds things up.

When the poem was almost complete I used to write it down longhand, but now I go straight to the computer.

Trink Hill

I have watched the flight of the white bird
I have seen the raven on the stone
I have heard the vixen calling to her young
I know the passage of the sun and moon

I have seen the raven on the stone
Egg shell, snail shell and brittle bone
I know the passage of the sun and moon
From the rising to the setting and beyond

Egg shell, snail shell and brittle bone
They come from dust and to dust they are gone
From the rising to the setting and beyond
From dawn till dusk and dusk till rosy dawn

They come from dust and to dust they are gone

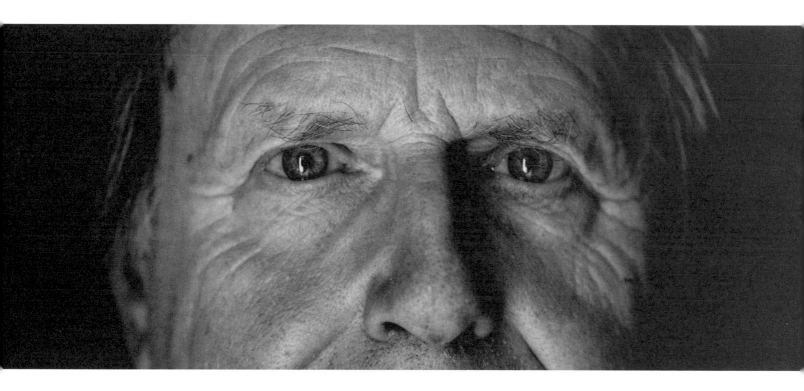

Mac Dunlop

Poet, Performer, Producer
Falmouth

I write all over. If I'm out and about and get an idea I'll head straight for a café to get it down. I've always got something to write with and a notepad or sketchbook; usually three or four on the go – bit of a mess really.

I need quiet. Music in cafés can be very distracting. I can zone out of conversation but music hooks. It is hard to find cafés without music. The library can be a good place.

My laptop gets fired up in the morning, often with a coffee and a sonnet. But it is also a terrible distraction – emails… I need stillness to write – so I try to get up early. Days are so busy and full, so first thing in the morning is often the only way. It's a good time to read too, a poem or two.

I do lots of drafts, arrows, crossings out. I try to keep a draft every time I make changes. If it is a longer piece there could be 18 or 19 versions. For shorter pieces I may just write over. That's convenient but at the same time you lose the archaeology of marks on the page.

I love the look of written pages scribbled over, crossed out, moved around. I'm also a visual artist and I like the way drawing and writing are intertwined in the act of mark making.

Generally it's somewhere in the house that I find my space. Annie and I work out where each is working. We also have a caravan. As a performance poet I do a lot of impromptu writing. When I'm writing for performance I work standing up, draft on the music stand, try it out, read aloud, re-draft, start again.

I use a smartphone sometimes to note down ideas. It's a quick way of trying out poems. My current radio series My Day Off is recorded using the phone.

I'm a sculptor, and draw too. I particularly like the way objects can evoke conversation out of nothing. Words are a material to me, like paint or clay.

Sculptural Fabrications by Mac Dunlop

An action for four voices in The Exchange Gallery in Penzance
(some answers contributed by gallery visitors)

I don't know what it means…
to be an artist?
to be black?
to be wrong?
to be deaf?

No… I don't know what it means…
to be beautiful?
to be straight?
to be normal?
to be happy?

No… I don't know what it means…
to be Syrian?
to be illegal?
to be me?
to be famous?

No… I don't know what it means…
to be content?
to be needed?
to be loved?
to be honest?

No… I don't know what it means…
to be smart?
to be big?
to be understood?
to be believed?
to be heard?

No… I don't know what it means…
to be right?
to be wrong?
to be grown up?
to be pregnant?

No… I don't know what it means…
to be yourself?
to be me?
to be extreme?
to be hungry?
to be thirsty?
to be rich?

No… I don't know what it means…
to be in love?

No! … I don't know what it
means…
to be from Mousehole?

Patrick Gale

Novelist
Sennen

The most important thing in a good writing space is a lack of distraction. A kind of silence, but with music, removed from everyday life. I have a purpose built writing room which my partner built for me on the farm. It was the bull's shed then a diesel store. For years I would write on the kitchen table or anywhere in the house. It is a beautiful oak-lined self-contained room about thirty seconds' walk from the kitchen but surrounded by garden. I have copies of my novels and reference books for my current project as well as photographs and linked objects. There is also a woodburner – I do need to be warm.

Most of my reading and research is done in the writing room. I actually enjoy writing outdoors (there is a bench just outside which catches the sun). I used to have a chaise longue but kept falling asleep. I work in longhand, sitting in a large armchair, using an Italian leather writing folder into which you can insert a hardback notebook. (I have several notebooks for each novel.) There are also useful pouches for chocolate bars! Typing up is then part of the process. I like to keep the creative process flexible for as long as possible. There is a desk with a long low window looking over the garden – it is deliberately low so that it can only be seen through when sitting down at the desk. I like to work office hours and start by nine. I may take a break in the afternoon but find I get a second wind after four.

A Place Called Winter.

From the first of five drafts by Patrick Gale

Earlier than that, before Hell, his memories were more damaged still. He remembered Paul vanishing and the sickening wait until they finally received a terse postcard from Saskatoon to say he had indeed enlisted there. He remembered Petra's extraordinary resourcefulness and resilience, insisting at once that he teach her all he knew so she could take her brother's place behind a plough or sowing a field. He remembered the one letter from Paul to reach them from France and then, weeks later, his being reported missing in action. He remembered. How could he not? He remembered the anguish of that not-quite-mourning, of grief muffled by the fluttering palm of hope. He remembered the harsh cure of hard work, less a cure than a numbing, and the sweet, sad distraction of his daughter's ignorance. And he knew the war was over and could even picture Winter's main street and new station building hung with flags in celebration.

Between that uncertain image, however, and his arrival here, lay rooms he couldn't enter. He knew they contained fear, guilt and a grief so powerful that even to put his hand on the doorknobs would fry his skin.

Rebecca Gregson

Novelist, Journalist, Content Writer
Mitchell

When the children were growing up, I wrote wherever I could, and the habit has survived the empty nest. I'm mostly peripatetic. A good space for me is one that is devoid of obligation with no reminders of the 'to do' list. It needs to be warm – I did try the garden shed once but it was freezing out there. It needs to be pleasing to the eye, so an interesting view or a comfy looking sofa, preferably someone else's. It also needs to be somewhere I don't have to think about getting interrupted. Home is problematic, mainly because I'm not very good at not offering tea to people who drop in out of the blue. I'd rather hide until whoever's car it is drives off again.

I have written many chapters in the back of my own car, sometimes parked in a layby or a school car park. This is just a time management issue. I always have my laptop with me so if I have half an hour to spare, I review and reflect on anything I've written. The back of the car is good because although I'd prefer to be outside, sitting in a field or something, it's difficult to see the screen. I have an estate car so there is space, focus and height. I must have done this at least once a week for the ten years or so the children were at school. It's not my preferred space but it worked at the time. I don't do it so much now.

The other thing I do is work in other people's houses. I am so easily distracted and cannot bear to be surrounded by my own cluttered life. To write Zebras Crossing I lived in a friend's flat in Brixton. For Eggshell Days, I took over another friend's vast dining room in Cornwall, me and my laptop at the end of a very long oak table. I am currently working on a first screenplay with another friend and we sit opposite each other at her much smaller table, in her cottage with incredible views of the Atlantic, surrounded by her clutter, her dog, not mine.

My daily life is not particularly structured – it's like that on purpose. If you are self-employed why not stay entirely flexible?

I do take great pleasure in what I do. With a novel I often start with the idea of a catalyst for change in someone's life. Then I develop the characters, relationships and plot their narrative trajectory. These characters are on a journey and I can't get interested until I know they have a destination.

Eggshell Days by Rebecca Gregson

A brush with mortality motivates a group of unfulfilled friends to swap London for Cornwall to renovate an inherited house. It gradually becomes apparent that there is no such thing as a quick fix, and friendships are fracturing. A bonfire, fuelled by bravado, gets out of control. Jonathan, teased for his disapproval, takes himself off to a small chapel in the grounds.

'The exposed wagon roof looked sound enough. The timber curved seamlessly, the distances between the beams were mathematically accurate, the edges of the wood were smooth. He tried to bring to mind the medieval carpenter who'd made it, a mason perhaps or an apprentice, but he couldn't summon anything more than a vague sense of rustic competence. His mind was locked, needing someone else's written word to form a mental image of anything. He patted the back pocket of his jeans, from which poked a few stapled pages.

A small wooden table sat below a large three-paned cinque-foiled leaded window, flanked by granite pillars set into the stone. There was a jam jar in the middle of the table, its insides stained with brown rings and floral debris.

He tried to conjure the chaplain too, but like the carpenter, he failed. Buildings he could see but people remained as text. Needing the security of someone else's knowledge, he pulled the pages from his pocket and started to read.

'Virtually all medieval buildings were constructed with lime. Lime was slower to build with, and required skill and patience, but produced durable, attractive and healthy results…'

He brushed his hands over the wall and bits fell out. Looking carefully at the internal pointing of the stones round the altar, he was interested in a large, clumsy patch of grey cement.

'Cement sets very hard and is impervious. Any moisture finding itself drawn in will be trapped and cause problems. Repairing lime-based buildings with lime-based materials is the answer…'

His hand went back to the crumbling mortar and his fingers rubbed the crevices. He didn't know how long he'd dug and scraped but by the time he walked back past the bonfire, Emmy and Niall had retreated to the house and the flames were just a gentle flicker.

Carl Grose

Playwright

Born in Truro, Cornwall. Based in Crystal Palace, London

I used to have my own writer's room, a private space to work, full of writer trinkets and talismans. I still have the stuff but not the room, as my two and a half year old son has requisitioned it now. With him in the world, I've learnt that I can't stay in the house to write. So I go out and find places. I wish I had done it before. It's a brilliant way to write. I find much more stimulus and focus this way. I live in Crystal Palace in South East London, so some days I work in the park café, purely so I can visit the dinosaurs (not a euphemism). The Crystal Palace dinosaurs are a legacy from the Great Exhibition.

The Crystal Palace itself was destroyed by fire in 1936 but the dinosaurs (built in 1854) look rather modern actually. Their proportions, however, are slightly "off" due to their creators working blindly from freshly found fossils. Because I see them pretty much every day, either heading to the café or walking my boy around, I've seen these beasts in many different lights. They live on an island surrounded (enclosed) by water – but I've seen them in snow, in thick mist, in the wet, autumn bleakness, in glorious morning sunshine, at dawn and at twilight. You can't see them at night because the park's closed – that's when they all come to life and rampage around, of course. I find them just so inspiring. They're big. Impressive. Historical. Inaccurate. Surreal. Apparently, they classify as the world's first theme park…

The café I work at is great. The staff there know me now. I'm a regular fixture most days. They sometimes ask questions about what I do, what I'm writing. They commiserate the lows and celebrate the highs of the writing life with me. I could be wrong but I think they like having a writer there. And as long as I force myself to buy some kind of all-day breakfast at lunchtime (the chorizo and scrambled eggs on rye is real good there) and keep topped up on flat whites they don't mind me staying all day. I have my seat. It's in the corner, at an old school desk, which somehow makes me work more studiously. I get somewhat antsy if someone's sat in my seat before me, but they soon move, especially if I stare at them hard enough. Before me at my desk is a big window, which is ideal for world-watching – as any writer will tell you, you need to be able to look up every now and then and watch the world outside pass by. It's a very gentle stimulus. Getting out of the house works well. As I said, I can't believe I didn't do it before. Working from home feels like too much of a distraction now.

Since having a child I've had to change the way I write… I can't get all arty and wait for the muse. I have to get on with it. My writing time has been chopped in half, so this fresh approach is born out of necessity. I've been re-learning how to work, and the conclusion I've reached is: hard and fast. But given that writing is mainly thinking, this is easier said than done. By going out somewhere, I do feel as if I have done a day's work. Writing at home, I rarely did.

In terms of objects at home I do have a wall of books on different topics and genres. I just like having them around. Some I've read, some I haven't. But they've all been bought for some once-urgent reason. Again, it's healthy stimulus. Books are great allies. Full of ideas. Plays. Novels. Reference books. Poetry. Comics. I love each and every one of them. Other artefacts include a few skeletons from Mexico, and a little Godzilla from Japan (here's me, back to big, scaly monsters again). I also have a vast collection of DVDs, hidden behind a lurid blue curtain. Films and books play a big part in my life.

I keep trying to evolve my process of writing. Initially, when I started off playwriting, I would research, keep a notepad, write lots of little bits, collect "ideas" for maybe a year and then sit down and attempt to write a play in two weeks. It took me a little too long to realise this approach didn't work for me. About ten years ago, I had an epiphany, and was gifted with an idea that almost wrote itself (these are rare, gold dust, and hardly ever appear like this). The intensity of the idea meant that I had very little say over how it came out, which was through dialogue. So I started very early on with dialogue, with the characters just talking to each other, and then after I'd gathered what I felt was enough, I started structuring it. I discovered all sorts of interesting things in the characters through their dialogue, things that I wouldn't necessarily have found in "ideas". They (the characters) led the story. It felt much more organic this way.

Now I'm in a new phase again, that's (I think) more of a considered approach with the two elements of dialogue and structure working in tandem. As a result, first drafts are a little closer to reaching the end result than previous ones.

I don't procrastinate – I don't have time. Even on the days I'm not working and have Arthur (my partner is an actor and is often performing, or rehearsing, or filming, or all three), I'll still write. I take my boy to the park, to check out the dinosaurs, and do some secret head writing. I have to grab every moment. There's so much to write and so little time.

49 Donkeys by Carl Grose

FADE TO:

Hank Williams: "Never Get Outta This World Alive".

FX: static interferes, breaks up the song...

BRAY   I was listenin to that!

           FX: another voice emerges from the radio crackle...

GROSE   ... so here I am, working on a play about a farmer who's hung 49 donkeys from trees on his farm and I'm talking to a guy who actually knows him –

           FX: BRAY skids to a sudden halt.

           SC 20: INT. GROSE'S HOUSE (STUDY). NIGHT.

GROSE   What are the chances of this happening? Of me meeting someone who's met Solomon Singo? A little more than 49 to 1, I can tell you. I was gobsmacked, cus, you hafto understand, here was someone who could answer the question that had been burning inside me all this time.

           (whispered)

           "Why? Why did he do it?" And Andalay shrugged and smiled, and said the reason why Solomon Singo hung those donkeys was because –

           FX: something crashes outside, almost too quiet for us to hear – but enough to set the dog off. This should make us JUMP!

GROSE   Christ! Lady! Frightened the life out of me!

           FX: LADY continues to bark.

GROSE   (walking)

           Alright, alright. I'll let you out.

           FX: chains, bolts – front door is opened.

GROSE   Go on, girl. Silly animal.

         FX: the dog shoots off into the night, barks diminishing. But continuing.

         With a yelp, the barks suddenly stop dead.

GROSE   Lady? Lady?

         FX: footsteps on gravel, approaching.

GROSE   Who the hell are you?

BRAY   You Carl Gross?

GROSE   Yes, I – actually, it's GROSE. G - R - O -

BRAY   I come all the way to Trura fer you. And I'll tell ya this fer nuthin, I 'ate Trura.

GROSE   What have you done with my dog?

BRAY   Dog's dead, mister. And you'll go the same way if you dun't gimme some answers!

GROSE   What?!

BRAY   Come on, sonny. Yer comin wimme!

         FX: DONK! GROSE collapses.

         SC 21: INT. BOSANKO FARM - KITCHEN. DAWN.

Alyson Hallett

Poet, Writer in Residence at Cyprus Well, Charles Causley's House 3/7/14 - 19/12/14
Launceston

Cyprus Well, Causley's house, is the most welcoming and easy place to work. It's drenched in Causley spirit; in the gentle, encouraging atmosphere that he created. There's a quality of quietness here that's really unusual. It's so intense it has a materiality – as if it's been made, day by day, year by year, forged in the furnace of the imagination.

Cyprus Well is a house that you step down into – literally and metaphorically. Two steps from the pavement into the little hall, then one more down into the front room. It's like entering another world. Even though I loved the house from the first moment that I arrived, I was quite nervous about staying here. I didn't know anyone in Launceston and six months can be a long time when you don't have many distractions. I needn't have worried: it's a kind, generous place and I thrived in it.

I was very conscious of the fact that it was Causley's home. I kept fresh flowers on his grave as a mark of respect and as an offering. I liked the ritual of walking to his grave, communing with him there as well as within the walls of his house. It felt important. A way of saying thank you for the generous legacy he'd left behind and for the chance to be a part of it.

One of the best days of the residency was spent visiting Causley's archive at Exeter University. It was amazing to see the depth and breadth of his work. His writing is fresh, startling, funny – it has made me look at my work again and open up borders that I didn't even know were there. Also, once, when I was looking through some editing I had done on my manuscript, I heard a voice say 'coming along nicely'. It wasn't the kind of thought I'd have. I think his gentle presence came through and encouraged me in the same way that he'd encouraged so many other poets.

I love to work in bed – by midday I'm surrounded by hundreds of books, mugs of tea, straight from sleep to work, crumbs, uncleaned teeth. Breaking all the rules! I also love working in Tesco's café – very anonymous. Very liberating. No conversation. It's a transient, terribly ordinary functional space. A good place to do editing.

I do procrastinate by doing the washing, sweeping the floor, playing Causley's piano, just getting out. Anything but write. But that's all part of it too. The doing and the not doing. The sleeping and the waking. The dreaming and the making. It all adds up in the end.

Orchard

After seeing him for the last time
I stumbled in among the apple
trees and fell down,
hands and knees in the dirt,
body shaking with the effort
of so much grief and shame
all at once.
I hoped the trees
would hide me,
shelter me from the people
drinking Pimms and laughing
in the sun. I wanted to burrow
down with the worms,
to have some anonymous gardener
heap bark-mulch and old leaves
on my back.
Small stones dug into my skin.
It was hard to believe
the man I'd just seen was him – so different,
so changed from the one I'd loved.
I wiped my face with my sleeve
as the six o'clock sun
careered towards pine tops
and a few white clouds sauntered
home. My tears soaked
down like rain,
turned dust to clod,
clod to something nutritious enough
for roots to suck back up again.

Seth Hampshire

Poet
Truro

I have a desk in my bedroom but I find it hard to sit down for too long, I end up getting fed up, drinking lots of coffee and so I get on my bike and go for a ride, out of town. It gets the blood flowing and by being outside and doing something physical, ideas come and the links between them.

I see writing as a series of islands and bridges – I know the islands I want to visit but sometimes I get stuck on an island. Going out on my pushbike or taking a brisk walk helps me figure out how to build a bridge to the next island.

My bike is a small green and grey BMX.

I like it because I can just jump off it at any time. I can throw it around, nip through town, jump off it and write things down as fast as I can on my mobile phone, then I can jump back on again.

I think movement helps to make my mind move on too. I've just got a motorbike and I tend to ride it over to the sea and the cliffs, where being out in the elements, the wind and the weather, really helps me to think and hear my thoughts.

I don't write things down, my notebook is my mobile phone most of the time, or on a laptop as it is easier to edit. I started to write much later in my life when I had things like a mobile or a computer, but I didn't really contact with writing at school, but I did make up fantasy stories as a child.

I took to writing as I got a bit older and things started to go wrong in my life, it gave me an outlet to clear my head. Now, when I want to write or need to clear my head, I take myself outside. I like being in the outdoors.

As for procrastination! I have four snakes and two lizards! One of my snakes is set up on my desk where, when I am not writing, I can spend happy time checking temperatures, cleaning them out and handling them. My snake collection consists of a Kenyan San Boa, Boa Constrictor, a Nelson Milk Snake and a Royal Python. The lizards are a Crested Gecko and a Rankin Dragon!

Lead Vest

sat on a branch, looking a little lost,
focused on her thoughts with fingers crossed,
head hung low staring straight through the fire,
her situation as odd as her chosen attire,

red shoes, white socks pulled to her knees,
brown skirt and jumper tight to fight the breeze,
her hair once tidy but now all a mess,
and beneath her jumper a thick lead vest,

she'd had a plan, and direction to go,
she hadn't tarried on her way but the process is slow,
and where five are needed but ten arrive,
half must find a way to survive,

she knew what she wanted and what to say,
but not what to do when turned away,
and this is when she acquired her new lead vest,
poisoned by problems they weigh heavy on her chest,

so sat on a branch ideas whirling through her head,
she longs to find a way to remove the garment made of
lead,
knowing while she wears it there's no way to flee,
but it can't be removed without a golden key

then paddling up the river came a boy with knotted hair,
and a smile on his face that said he had not a single care,
she called out to him but he seemed not to hear,
she shouted again but his ignorance became clear,
she trudged to the river's edge but slipped in the mud,
and came to the ground with an almighty thud,
the loud sound grabbed the boy's attention,
he angled his boat and paddled in her direction,

he came to the bank exactly where she lay,
thrust out his hand and asked would you like to play,
she took his hand but looked confused at what he said,
oh silly me he muttered how can you wearing lead,

he pulled her to her feet and jumped back in his boat,
I'd invite you in he said but I have a feeling we won't float,
I know what you need though I can find a golden key,
just walk up the river until you find my poem tree,

oh and just a final word before I really have to leave,
pixies may seem kind my friend but do not be deceived,
and then he turned his back and went on up the stream,
alone she stood and watched until ripples could not be
seen,

then clutching at her hope she turned and began to walk,
she hadn't gone far when she heard someone talk,
not much further again she saw the light of a dying fire,
and the voices close as sweet as an angelic choir,

perched on dry logs talking over the embers,
she saw the pixie council and all its seven members,
she tried to go unseen but her heavy steps could not be
masked,
she remembered the boy and she remembered her task,

she remembered the warning but it was hard to believe,
these lovely little faces were not what she'd perceived,
come and sit with us take the weight off your feet,
we'll start the fire again and make you food to eat,

you needn't stay long just sit for a little while,
you look so tired love as though you've walked a mile,
and in that heavy vest one mile's a long way,
it's evening now dear, you've done enough today,

their offer was appealing it was more than she could ask,
she moved toward their logs and quickly forgot her task,
she sat down near the fire and listened to them chat,
she ate the food they gave until she was close to feeling
fat,

she sat a while longer before her eyelids fell
and on that log she slept under the pixie spell,
when her eyes opened she found herself alone,
back to square one, lost in the great unknown,

the fire was no more the logs were all gone,
she knew what'd happened what had gone wrong,
she raged at herself, furious in her mind,
the boy had been right the pixies were not kind,

she'd listened to his warning, it had not gone ignored,
but caught up in the moment she'd been dragged
onboard,
and quickly lost her drive while forgetting all her haste,
but the plans that were made were not yet a waste,

so searching for the stream she started out again,
dreaming of the poem tree and her only friend,
trying her best to cover the land that remained,
she walked on with eyes peeled and ears strained,

she listened so hard, she mistook sounds for her desires,
and everywhere she looked she could see distant fires,
at first she almost cried with sudden alarm,
but realising the trickery she fought to keep calm,

one step at a time, because that's all she could consider,
and somehow she found her way back to the river,
then following it up she continued her procession,
searching for what had now become her obsession,

and then in the distance she saw the curious tree,
and the boy with knotted hair down on one knee,
a shovel in hand carefully digging out the weeds,
secateurs on the ground for cutting dead leaves,

as she neared, he became aware of her arrival
I'm so glad to see you, I was concerned for your survival,
there are many tricks he said many traps to get caught in,
nothing's certain in these woods when you're out walking,

you start working he said I will retrieve your prize
and he passed her the shovel with delight in his eyes,
she continued his labours as he darted behind the tree,
and she didn't stop until he returned with the key,

you did it he exclaimed and I am so impressed,
many never manage to remove their lead vest,
she slid the key in the lock and turned it with all her might,
 as the vest fell to the ground she was filled with delight,

she stood and rolled her shoulders leant down to stretch
her back,
slowly stood and turned to look at her fresh track,
then took the secateurs and continued with her work,
no longer paying mind to the woods where the pixies lurk.

Pol Hodge – Mab Stenek Veur

Poet – Bardh
Grampound Road

My coats have many pockets and in each is a folded piece of paper I carry everywhere I go to write down anything interesting – this one has the outline of the legend of St Breock. I think in Cornish so all my notes are in Cornish. The magic of translation can only happen after coffee…

I've got hundreds of bits of paper which then get filed and then 'knocked up' in red pen on another bit of paper. I've got the genesis of poems on the back of paracetamol packets and Macdonald's receipts. I keep the rough notes on me then work on finding the rhyme and syllable count. I'm good at tweaking and making the language scan, say to fit to music. I write anywhere and everywhere but my office (sodhva) is the place where I write it up fitty.

Every wall is lined with books including a full set of An Gannas – the all Cornish monthly that has been running since 1972. Lots of dictionaries and a handwritten rhyming dictionary which I've compiled – but I am not a slave to rhyme. I need my books in case I need to investigate something further.

Once the poem is typed up, I print it off and put it in the rough file folder, then hopefully they will end up as a book. I have a collection waiting to go now. I then translate them into English if worth doing. I sometimes use a dijen of dialect as well.

Mordonn by Pol Hodge

My a wel an gorwel glas,
genesigva, mor ow thas,
hwythans ov y'n keynvor bras.

My a glyw oll ow hwerydh,
ni yw milvil ilewydh
ow kul an mordros nowydh.

My a vlas goemmon ha men,
ynwedh diwedh ow thremen
ha'm mernans y'n bys mabden.

My a dav tir a'y dewes
hag yth ov vy dinerthhes
ha na moy dhe omglywes.

Seawave

I see the blue horizon,
birth-place, a sea my father,
I am a gust in the big ocean.

I hear all my sisters,
we are a million musicians
making the new sound of the sea.

I smell seaweed and stone,
also an end to my time
and my death in mankind's world.

I touch land and its sand
and I am de-energised
and no more to feel.

Mark Jenkin

Screenwriter, Filmmaker
Newlyn

What I like about this space is that it's my space – I can't write at home. I need to be alone. It is really quiet but there are other artists' studios around so there is company if I need it. I have access to the outside; I wouldn't use it half as much if I couldn't wander in and out. There is no wifi and the phone reception isn't great – so there aren't a lot of distractions. I think I could actually live here – I've got a camping stove, a toothbrush and sleeping bag, and there's a toilet next door.

I like to get here really early when I can. I work well in the morning and then slow down. In fact I may even sleep in the armchair or on the floor for a bit in the afternoon. If I have a deadline, I work full on. I work best with a deadline.

As I work a lot with film, which is a tactile material, I work standing up. All the editing on the computer is done standing up too – in the old fashioned way. If I'm writing I like to put a cushion on the floor and work down there.

I never write with a computer. I used to write into a notebook but now I write on loose sheets of paper all over the floor. These I can then cut up and re-order, lay them out in a linear, circular or fragmented style. It's a process that's still in development but I think it complements the chaos of the mind. When I am happy with what I have I'll type it up, which forces me to re-write.

I once made a film which I edited and then it was accidentally deleted and I had to start again. It was two years work lost but the film was better for it in the end. Like a lot of people I tend to protect and accumulate but actually everything that is valuable is in your head, you can't lose it. All the rubbish goes if you recreate a second time as you are focussed on the end point and can get rid of everything that doesn't work.

I've got everything in here that I think I may use some day. Books are very important as a resource but also as a physical distraction. I've got a record player that I love. A while ago I converted all my music to MP3 but then I never listened to it again. I couldn't get my head around it. There was nothing physical there to spark the interest. Putting on an album has a certain ritual about it and I like to really listen. Listening to music properly is like reading a book. Similarly I've gone back to using film as much as possible in my work. I understand it and am not leaving creative decision making to a computer or automated camera. I mix all the chemicals myself and process the film by hand in a small developing tank – it takes up to an hour per hundred feet of film, so you have to be committed to what you are doing. I've created methods that are work intensive but for me the work is nothing unless you've struggled with it.

I do procrastinate but I think it is really valuable; it's clearly part of the process, a large percentage of work is procrastination. I listen to music, tidy up, stare at the wall. I buy things that are loosely related to the project in hand, like tracking down a particular book, however obscure. If I'm writing, I might do other bits of filmmaking. I watch DVDs or old VHS tapes. I don't do much that isn't related to work, however spurious the link.

Narcissi, from Aurora's Kiss by Mark Jenkin

On the 4th September he told me,

"There's nothing but empty, whistling, nothingness.

I'm searching for words beyond the end of a thought."

He said, "Don't ask me about excitement and expectation.

There is none today."

We walked to the fields above the town where the narcissi grew, though there were none that day. Only the discarded rubber bands from the previous harvest.

He told me that as kids they did cartwheels up here wearing kaleidoscope sunglasses. He said that he often dreamed that she'd return once the narcissi bloomed and wondered whether maybe she still had the glasses, to see 50 visions of him all at once.

Excitement, and expectation, whether he liked it or not, for a moment there was some.

Mercedes Kemp

Writer, Educator and Director of Research and Community with Wild Works
Carnyorth

I see myself as an ideas generator. I have a very visual approach and create words which promote an image. From these provocations we make theatre. We translate the real world into a heightened image. This is fabulation – the process of close observation of the world through heightening it.

In my space I have so many rituals. I also have many spaces. In my house, upstairs I have my hermit place for ideas and writing. I am very fussy – if anyone else is in the house I can't work. It is a very solitary business. I also have a big office at the University where there is a beautiful light and here I do the 'roll up your sleeves stuff' – re-writing and proposals, describing and advocating for projects.

I am also interested in the in-between spaces like trains or doctors' surgeries. In Malta I did a lot of work in the doctor's waiting room – I find they become very thoughtful spaces, even if they are loud they feel quiet. You have total anonymity and nothing else to do.

I find writing on the production site the hardest. Very often some writing is required immediately. I have lots of notebooks where I write by hand but this can be quite hard, especially if it is wet, as everything dissolves.

I'm always writing. It's different by hand as it's slower.

In the last few years I've started writing more poetry and become very interested in the layout of work and its links to audiences and publications – text in space, two words per line which tempt you to read on. I've enjoyed the internal rhythm which is so different from prose.

I craft a lot in my head – I'm not a massive re-drafter.

In my writing room I have some books and access to the internet. So much of what I do is research-based. I create massive files which are the core of the research and from that the work expands and evolves.

My house is full of objects. In my room I have my book collection. I keep accruing bits and pieces.

I find procrastination an amazing virtue and very productive. I'm big on this and allowing for failure. Time for thinking and putting something to the back of my mind. This is accepted now in the arts.

I do a lot of thinking while walking my dog on the cliffs at Botallack. I love the massive horizons and feel suffocated if not by the sea.

Charlotte at The King's Staircase by Mercedes Kemp, 2010

Consider this girl
with her scabby knees
and her rider's gait
and her wild hair.
Picture this mutinous girl
with her dogs
and her horses
and her retinue of guardians who are picked
because they don't like children very much.
They all fall in love with this child
and are quickly sacked
to make room for more child-haters.
And who does the hiring?
Her papa, who would be king,
but is no prince charming.
A toad prince, in fact
whom no-one will ever kiss that way
and so, remains a toad
with no love in his heart
for the young princess.
There were no fairies invited at her christening
although some say
they detected
a shadowy presence.

When she was born
her father
had her locked away
in a house in the forest
looked after by the endless stream
of loveless attendants.
She grew up quite the wild child
climbing up trees with her skirts
tucked into her knickers,
riding horses bareback
and running,
always running
towards the gates
of the forest house,
or dancing in the woods
alone?
by moonlight
The time of reckoning is coming.
She is, after all
the only princess
of the Royal Blood.
She must be married,
and it is her father
the Toad Prince

who will do the choosing.
A prince is brought across the seas
to meet her.
He is hideous.
And so she runs.
She is filled with strangeness.
She must run
like so many girls before her
into the arms of love.
He's tall and handsome.
He wears a white uniform.
He's fresh from the wars.
He awaits at the bottom of the stairs
with a happily-ever-after smile.
All might be well.
But all the clocks in the palace stop.
The princess is poised motionless
in mid-leap.
Now, we already know
that there were no fairies at her christening
and that a shadowy presence was seen to be
loitering.
The princess WILL fall

into the arms of the beloved.
She will be happy,
for a while.
On her wedding day there will be angels passing,
gods pronouncing,
sages advising
and crowds strewing the roads with roses
red as desire.
But the shadowy form has always been behind her.
She was running towards love
and dancing with death all her life.

Liz Kessler

Author for Children and Young Adults
St Ives

I wanted a sofa bench by the window so I can sit here and look out of the window, with a second table so I can work by hand if I need to, as well as at my computer. I wanted to create somewhere where you walk in and it feels creative, where I can come up with stories, relax and be open to ideas… This is the best space I have ever had – quiet, gentle, my heart feels at rest, it has my books, the things I have done, letters from eight year old readers… To get here you have to go through two doors and up some stairs, so it is another world, my space, and a place to work. I spent months getting it right and everything has been made specially. I think it has the most stunning view over St Ives Bay.

It is very new, so I've only edited my most recent novel 'Read Me like a Book' here and started my new one, which is called 'Haunt Me'. The experience with this new book is like nothing I've experienced before – it feels more creative. The space makes the process seem less like a job.

I normally spend about three months working on a plot until I have a very in-depth plot line. Then I write. But this time it seems like it has gone up a gear.

I have a playlist on my phone linked to the story which I listen to when walking the dog and the characters and story develop before my eyes as I walk.

I have a special notebook for each book – it needs to be the right notebook. The early stages are all handwritten and then typed up and printed off. I then cut it up and move the pieces around until there is a clear narrative. Only then will I actually write the novel.

My main procrastination is the internet; I call Twitter the writers' staffroom… I also create long term timetables for completion, including a target number of words a day – usually two thousand. This helps me to feel safe and makes it achievable. I don't always stick to it but then I can revise my plan. The challenge is to meet deadlines and keep my publisher and readers happy, whilst simultaneously staying true to my vision and creativity.

From The Tail of Emily Windsnap by Liz Kessler

Published by Orion Children's Books

I reached out but couldn't get hold of the ladder. What had I done? My legs were joining together again, turning to stone! I gasped and threw my arms about uselessly, clutching at nothing. Just cramp, just cramp, I told myself, not daring to look as my legs disappeared altogether.

But then, as rapidly as it had started, something changed; I stopped fighting it.

OK, so my legs had joined together. And fine, now they had disappeared completely. So what? It was good. It was... right.

As soon as I stopped worrying, my head stopped slipping below the surface. My arms stopped flailing about everywhere. Suddenly I was an eagle, an aeroplane – a dolphin, gliding through the water for the sheer pleasure of it.

Right, this is it. You might have guessed by now or you might not. It doesn't matter. All that matters is that you promise never to tell anyone.

I had become a mermaid.

Philip Marsden

Writer
The Roseland

"You never regret a baby or a swim." Russian saying.

I have a purpose-built writing room in the field next to our garden. My father was an architect and we put a lot of thought into getting it just right. It is quiet and solidly built and a physical distance from the house – I need to walk through the veg garden to get here. It has a different orientation to the house which adds to the apparent distance.

It's not a big space but is somehow self-contained. There is no internet – just a lot of books. It is purely for reading and writing – and thinking. All the business element of my life, the bills and admin and stuff – that's done from a desk in the house.

I like to work from early in the morning, first thing. In the winter it's still dark. I find I work better in winter – less light helps to set the imagination a-whirr, and makes the act of sitting in a chair less burdensome. In the summer there are too many wonderful things to do to be hunkered all day inside, writing.

The space needs to be warm: there's a certain sort of acute stillness that writing requires – not just sitting but sitting in a state of poised readiness. It's not something you notice yourself doing, until suddenly you find you've cricked your neck. That sort of stillness can also make you pretty cold.

I walk a lot and part of the process of writing is taking notes as I walk. There is a richness and immediacy from such notes which can't be created in a writing space. Back indoors I can craft, refine, re-write. But however much the prose depends on the outdoors, on scribbling notes, on travel to far-off places, I still find the most rewarding part of the entire production is here, in the writing room, watching it all take shape, seeing language reveal its alchemy and magic and perform its extraordinary tricks.

From Rising Ground: A Search for the Spirit of Place by Philip Marsden

Granta Books 2014

The next day, I left early to walk south across Bodmin Moor. Mist covered everything, wrapping its grey limbs around the shoulders of the hills, filling the valleys – until the sun rose and it vanished. Then there was the A30 to cross at Jamaica Inn and a bit of road-walking, and a couple of dull blocks of conifer plantation. But my memory of that day is not of those things. It is of the endless open, the bare expanses of grassland, a flock of curlew rising near Kilmar Tor, a ruined farm at Rushyford, weed waving in a stream, tormentil in the spongy sward, the warm wind, and that sense of intoxication that comes from too much sun, too much empty space, or too much time spent on your own – in this case, all three.

I followed no path. I crossed lines of grassy banks, passed low mounds. A cuckoo put its two-note query to the morning. On the edge of Craddock Moor, I stood over a sheep's carcass: the head was gone and the blood-crusted trachea flopped out over the neck. I puzzled at numerous lumps of granite – and began to identify various coffin-size boulders that had not been arranged by gravity.

Once you think you see one Neolithic 'propped stone', you see them everywhere. You spot design in the clitter-falls, deliberate curves on the open terrain, shapes in the clouds. Something about the blankness of the moor makes you react against it and fill it with significance – or anything. I remembered a passage in an essay by Jonathan Raban. He was sailing for the first time off the Pacific coast when his depth sounder suddenly showed the water shallowing. The sea-bed was rising towards him. A group of rocks? Shoals? Grabbing his chart, he checked his position. Rather than shallowing, he saw that the bottom had in fact dropped off the edge of the continental shelf. Faced with nothing, the sonic pulses were turning the tiniest speck into something solid.

Callum Mitchell

Poet, Theatre Maker
Newlyn

At present, I work from home in a cosy studio flat situated on the seafront between Newlyn and Penzance. It's big enough that there is a divide between where I sleep and where I write, but I enjoy being in close proximity to my bed. I don't sleep a huge amount, but knowing that my bed is nearby encourages me to keep going if I am flagging. If I were in an office I would constantly be thinking about getting home.

I begin writing very early in the morning, as soon after first light as possible. I am far more efficient at this time. I shower, eat breakfast and then go for a walk along Newlyn Green with a coffee and a cigarette. Once at my desk, I will try and write for around six hours, only stopping for quick breaks in between. I tend to have several projects on the go at one time. I prefer it this way. I get bored easily and I'm terrible at finishing ideas but love starting them. There is nothing more exciting than an empty page. I don't really believe in writer's block but I do procrastinate a fair bit. Usually this means tidying up. I need to have a nice clean space to work in. Deadlines are incredibly useful too. It helps to inject a bit of panic, otherwise I'd spend all day watching clips of Jake Thackray on YouTube.

I like to be surrounded by everything I need: books, stereo, coffee, tobacco. If I do listen to music while I'm writing, it tends to be mostly instrumental. Too much going on in the background it distracts me. My current favourites to write to are a duo called A Winged Victory For The Sullen and my friend Fluff's band, Eleven Magpies.

I am trying more and more to write first drafts by hand these days. I think typing straight onto a laptop can trick you into thinking a piece is better than it is, just because it looks nice on the screen. I try not to self-edit or labour over the text as I go. I want to get it all out as quickly as possible, have a break from it, and then revisit and edit with fresh eyes. This process can alter slightly depending on what I'm working on. If it's a poem I will do a lot more wandering, listening to music and try not to force it too much. It's about finding the rhythm. Often, the majority of the piece will be rattling around in my head for several days before I write any of it down. When I am devising shows with Silly Boys, it is a much more collaborative experience. We usually start with an outline of a story and lots of ideas and then spend a couple of weeks improvising. I will go home after rehearsals each night and type up a script by looking at videos we have recorded from the sessions.

I Come From

From 'Always Changing, Forever The Same', a mixed-media show about the village of Newlyn, created by people living and working in the village. By Callum Mitchell

I come from a village that time forgot.

From cobbled streets, lilting cottages and lopsided chimneys that burp clouds of wood-smoke. I come from creased flesh and Cornish whispers, creaking paddles and upturned punts. I come from fantasy and folklore, shanties and legend. From knockers and piskies and buccas and saints.

I come from a land that's always changing and yet forever the same.

A second-home-owner's sordid fetish. A city slicker's wet dream. From bobbing boats and inky black seas to ashtray grey shorelines of pebbles piled up like towers of copper coins. Where bare-chested blokes slug ale and sweat dirtbar, and stilletoed songbirds stilt-walk along harbour walls. I come from pink sunsets and silhouetted seagulls, all swooping and scavenging, ducking and diving. I come from a family that works fingers to the bone, till bones are brittle and can take no more.

I come from bathtubs full to the brim, all five of us piled in, with barely a bar of soap between us.

I come from carwashes, jumble sales and Christmas Carols in June… Anything to earn a bit of extra pocket money… I come from bows and arrows, catapults and cardboard armour. From Nutella sandwiches, no money for a lunchbox, odd socks and basin haircuts. I come from mud-slides and pile-ons, pier dives and Jelbert's Ice Cream.

I belong to a faded memory. A melancholy. A nostalgia. A dream.

It's in my blood. Thick as fish guts.

This land is my land. My story. My myth. My home.

Graham Mitchell

Scriptwriter
Falmouth

I've just moved into this house in Falmouth and the sitting room is to become my writing room… it has views over the river! In our last house I worked in a shed a friend made for me.

My two favourite places for writing or gathering ideas are cafés and trains. In particular the 18.03 Pullman Carriage, the restaurant car from Paddington to Cornwall. There are two extraordinary restaurant managers, social engineers, who I'm convinced pair up strangers they think will fire off each other. You can't just sit and eat in silence; you have to talk to people you don't know. I've met some extraordinary people – a Bollywood actor, a foreign correspondent, a head hunter, a spy. People really open up – they think we'll never meet again.

I've always worked from home, normal office hours from nine till six. I can't do it any other way. I just need a desk, computer, books, paper, sometimes post-it notes. I work to commission, sometimes writing episodes for an existing TV series or pitching my own ideas. If it is my own work then there is a longer development phase. I have to strike the balance between creating something that's commercial but that also has something to say.

I have a theatre background, both acting and writing, which I suppose is why I love the collaborative nature of scriptwriting. I get to create a big canvas then give it up to the director and production team to realise it. I've learned to let go of ownership and it excites me watching other people bring themselves to the work and bring it alive.

Writing for TV is like tissue paper – it's there and then it's gone. But it can have enormous impact – in that place and time.

From The Catch, by Graham Mitchell

EXTERIOR SHOTS OF MOUNTS BAY/NEWLYN HARBOUR - DUSK

Cornwall. The sea black in the falling darkness. Inside the harbour, the water's calm. Rusting trawlers and crabbers, netters and day boats. Drizzle hangs in the harbour lights. Crews in oilskins load and off-load pots and nets.

INTERIOR SHOTS OF THE SWORDFISH. BAR. NEWLYN - DUSK

A wash of voices and piped music. We're tight on a wall, a nicotine-stained print of a crude 19th century painting hanging there: men in breeches, striped tops and Wee-Willy-Winkie hats unload barrels by lantern light on to a night time beach. The inscription:

> Five and twenty ponies trotting through the dark,
> Brandy for the parson, baccy for the clerk,
> Laces for a Lady, letters for a spy
> And watch the wall, my darling, while the gentlemen go by.

We're in a public bar. It used to be spit and sawdust, now there's lino on the floor but little else has changed. The place is rammed with fishermen.

TOMMY GEORGE (late 30s, weather-beaten and powerful, dressed in oilskins) is standing at the bar with STEVE PENROSE (also late 30s in jeans and cowboy boots) and MIGSY (a boyish-faced guy in his 50s wearing shorts and wellies).

STEVE   Migsy sold me what he had flat rate.

TOMMY   (re Steve) Flat rate to that bastard.

STEVE   (laughing) Oi, oi..

MIGSY   He bought the whole bleddy catch.

TOMMY   What you get per kilo?

               Migsy looks to Steve who doesn't say.

               (Re Migsy) Won't say will 'ee cos you know you been 'ad.

               Tommy's daughter, TESS (19, also in oilskins), joins them putting an empty glass down.

TESS   It's cos your brain's still new, in't it Migs? You see the best in everybody.

Annamaria Murphy

Poet, Playwright, Short Story Writer and Workshop Queen
Paul, near Mousehole

A good writing space for me requires a firm desk with room for me to lay out my notebooks and scrapbooks. A comfortable chair. Preferably, somewhere away from home: a shed, a café … I was nine years old when I was inspired by hearing an interview with Roald Dahl on the radio where he described having a shed in his garden with his notebooks, pictures and objects which helped him write his stories. This became a mythical shed in my head… and now I've got one in my garden!

Ideally I would like virtually nothing in it but the reality is that it is full of stuff – too full. Ironically, it is mainly resource and project materials for encouraging writing in schools. I do have a pinboard with postcards and bits of writing, also posters about print. And I have books of art and photography. Very particular ones. When I get fed up with looking at words, I look at them. I like the fact that I don't have the internet there.

I usually put off the actual moment of writing for as long as I can. I may go for a walk with my notebook, make a scrapbook or make a story box of objects. Only then will I start writing. I then give myself deadlines – or they are imposed.

My procrastination activities are part of my process but there is also desk tidying and making another cup of tea…

Friday Night in Launceston by Annamaria Murphy, courtesy of Kneehigh Theatre Rambles Project

Hicks and Sons, twin sets and cashmere,
Handbags and haberdashery,
Former underwear glories
And the peel of gold lettering.
Reflections of young girls
And older ladies,
Caught forever in the glass,
Who once looked longingly at lingerie and stockings.
The mannequins flinch slightly at
Youth who gather at the war memorial,
Just as Tanya, security guard in scarlet lipstick
And orange tan takes her position
Outside The White Hart,
Its gilt letters now say
"Whit art ote".

Polish workers emerge from taxis ,
A blonde leg dangles from the back seat.
Evensong at St.Mary's and karaoke from the Old Belle
Make a
Strange symphony.
"Don't encroach on the war memorial", says the sign,
And nobody does.
In the square,
A place for gathering ,
The young are a flock of rooks,
Preening their going out feathers with the mating call,
"Going Bude?"
Gorgeous girls flutter chiffon wings and shiver in the
cool.

In Sagor's Indian restaurant,
There's only us as lounge music
Plays to the sizzle of Masala.
Business slow for a Friday night
Waiters polite and shuffling,
The closed sign turns as soon as we leave.

Down the hill,
Past the crumble of castle, lovers in the bushes,
Past John Coles, photographer,
Taker of family and "Boudoir" photographs,

Past the Railway Inn, where we dare not enter, the
memory of nicotine,
A flicker of football from wide screen.

In the Rose Bed and Breakfast,
The proprietor's husband ,
A worn out sheet of a man,
Shuffles under the weight of crocheted
Tissue box covers and cooked breakfasts.
That night,
In the shadow of the castle
And the beauty of its streets,
I join the sleepless of Launceston.

Next morning,
In the granite coloured mizzle,
We meet at Cyprus Well,
Charles Causley's house.
Wallpaper peeling,
The must of old slippers,
Haunted by words
Tell me tell me Sarah Jane
My young man's a Cornishman
Timothy Winters Lord, Amen,
We see his suit hanging on a doorway,
Still pressed,
 And a pair of shoes,
Ordered from Harrods,
Still wrapped in tissue,
Possibly never worn by
That Gentle Man.

Simon Parker

Playwright, Journalist, Publisher
Linkinhorne

It's good to have a proper room. Mine is typically cluttered, with shelves of books, a collection of 45s and CDs, rocks picked up on beaches and mountains, an iPod dock and record player, family photographs, theatre fliers, whisky, chocolate biscuits. The desk is one I used at the old Western Morning News offices back in the 1980s. It's huge and ancient and made of oak. Everything was chucked out when the building, with all its ghosts of hacks and printers and stories, was demolished. But the desk survives. It's big enough to accommodate computers and notebooks and pencils and all the rest of the paraphernalia needed for writing and for book publishing.

I have to work quickly for newspapers (interview… type… publish… chip paper), but I write quite slowly when working on drama. Gonamena took years to cook. Seven Stars and A Star On The Mizzen also bubbled away for ages. Mad Dog, The Illegible Bachelor, Solid, Fourteen Seconds and Horses Stood Still were quicker. When working on a full-length play, I begin with a strong, universal theme. For Third Light, it was the notion of 'luck' – good and bad. For months this little room became a jumble of research materials: my lucky grandfather's First World War memoirs, first-hand interviews with elderly people in the 'fortunate' village of Herodsfoot, a ton of history books, music scores (Malcolm Arnold's Four Cornish Dances, Simon Dobson's Clarion Alarum, my son Tom's Thirteen Men) and recordings. Music has always been central to all that I do.

But is this room where the plays get written? I'm not sure. Some of the grunt work, the research, the editing and so on, is done here, but often the best bits arrive on walks or driving or when I should be doing something else entirely, with the help of a pencil, note book and, sometimes, dictaphone.

As well as my own room, I can use a friend's shack. It has a bed and a table, but no phone or internet or view, so there are few distractions. If I need to finish a play, that's where I go, working night and day until it's done, with lots of coffee and biscuits and music. I finished Gonamena and Third Light in the shack. The ideas and most of the dialogue were already in place, but the isolation helped to clarify the narrative and hone the structure. Unlike pencils, which are necessities, the shack and my room are luxuries. And I feel lucky to have the use of them.

THIRD LIGHT

Act 1 Scene 5

SFX

RECORDED VOICE

They was as good as we was. We nipped over the top and went as fast as we could go and dropped down. If Gerry was gone, he was gone, and if he wasn't you had to frighten him out from where he was.

BUZZ makes a chicken noise from where he has ended up sat at the front of the stage. BERT is holding a battered teddy bear. He looks at it, thoughtfully. He cradles it.

BERT   You ever held a baby?

        BUZZ looks at him quizzically.

BUZZ   A what?

BERT   A baby. New born. Fresh from its mother's womb. Never held mine 'til much later. Wasn't done back then for the man to hold the baby so soon. I held Charlie's grandson last week, mind. Two days old. Quiet as the moon he was. You'll need a firm hand, I told Charlie. Hold them tight across the chest and they feel secure, content. Leave 'em loose and they'll bawl the house down.

BUZZ   How are you telling me this just now?

BERT   I was just thinking.

BUZZ   About Charlie?

BERT   Uh-huh. He taught me how to live again when I come home from over there. Should've been the other way round, mind. Me teaching him, like. Some days I still want to tell him what it was like over to France, Buzz. What we saw. I've tried, but it's all history to the young… someone else's history.

        Pause.

BUZZ   'Ow's he doing?

BERT   Charlie? All right, he's all right. Still working over Liskeard market. Got a nice little place down by the station. Reckons he'll be retiring in a couple of year.

BUZZ   Geddon. You're boy an old age pensioner. What's that make us, old pal?

BERT   Ready for the knacker's yard, I reckon.

Pause.

BERT   Stan always reckoned it was the same with a rifle.

Long pause.

BUZZ   What?

BERT   Holding a baby! Keep up, man. That's what Stan reckoned. 'That gun can be slippy as a frog,' he'd say. 'If we've any chance of coming out of this in one piece, you'll have to grip that rifle close to your chest and run Gerry's line like a long-dog after a rabbit.'

Pause.

BUZZ   He was right, too. From kick-off to final whistle. Poor Stan.

BERT goes off on a ramble.

BERT   Something to live for, see. A baby. Never saw my Charlie 'til I come home, mind, but I had such a yearning to meet the little chap. Four year old. He knew me right away. Soon's I come striding down the hill. His mother had told'n all about his Da. And she never left hold of hope. She knew me and Charlie'd be best pals. And she was right. As always. Knowing I 'ad to get back to him was what kept me going. 'Twas Charlie saved me from the Kaiser's bullets. And Stan, of course.

BUZZ   Poor old Stan. Always the best of us.

BERT nods in earnest.

BERT   Best man in Herodsfoot village. Best man in St Pinnock parish, I reckon. Whole of blimmin' Cornwall, I shouldn't wonder.

BUZZ   Steady on. It's Stanley Doney we're on about, not Stanley Matthews.

Pause.

BERT   It was he got us into that mess in the first place, mind.

BUZZ   Gyah, we'd have gone anyhow.

Jane Pugh

Writer, Teacher, Editor, Narrative Obsessive
Penzance

I don't have a specific writing space – Hemingway was a bit sniffy about writing spaces, he felt a writer should be able to write anywhere. I enjoy the counterpoint of quite noisy places where you are forced to concentrate. I visit a café, find a table that doesn't wobble and I scribble away, using cheap stationery so I'm not bothered if I spoil it. I prefer writing on to the computer. I went on a really boring secretarial course when I was young and learned to touch-type. It was worth it, touch-typing is so liberating – it means you can write as fast as you think, and I love old typewriters.

If I take a notebook out with me I can never think of any ideas, my mind goes blank. So I deliberately don't take one and either write on my hands and arms or trust in my memory. If something is important I will remember it. And it's brilliant fun thinking of ideas.

I am a brutal editor and love the process of editing. Shaw said "I wanted to write you a short letter but didn't have the time." My ambition is to say a lot with a little. Writing for me is re-writing; editing is very important. I take notes from others and don't look for compliments but if they come my way, I'm very happy to take them. I love pleasing an audience. Love it.

My reason for moving to Cornwall is that it is so varied, creative and people have so much energy and drive; they make things happen. I worked in film and TV for a long time. I learned my discipline in TV. You can't sit and wait for inspiration, you have to crack on as a cast and crew is standing, waiting for a script. I like to work office hours: a seven-hour working day. If I start late, I'll work late.

I suppose the sea is my writer's space. Swimming is a physical manifestation of writing – I stand at the side, plunge in, am submerged then reach the surface again. It represents a perfect narrative arc: the hero stands on the side ready to embark on her journey, she plunges in – the adventure begins, she swims – the adventure unfolds; will she surface? That's the tension and the drama. She emerges and that's the resolution. Story is as simple and as beautiful as that – which is why, having read thousands of scripts and stories for my work, I never tire of it.

But I do procrastinate by walking the dog, wiping surfaces – if you have to house share, share with writers or out of work actors, your home will always be clean. I love cuddling up with a box set. I'm not interested in objects – just my fridge, coffee pot and patient, loyal dog at my side.

From The Adventurers by Jane Pugh

The story is set in St Agnes during the height of the copper mining industry – 1860s. A boy, 14, MATTHEW, stands on stage wearing a distinctive black cap. Behind him the brass bands sit in shadow but are then illuminated when playing.

CHAPTER ONE: The Mines Are the Universe to Accompany 'From the Earth'

MATTHEW delivers his soliloquy on the earth and industry. He is a clever, vibrant and cheerful boy but delivers his soliloquy with a sense of foreboding.

MATTHEW

What is the greatest of all?

In chapel on fresh Sundays, the minister says it is God

In our village of tight-fitting, cobbled street cottages, the neighbours say it is love

But neither is so.

It is the bleddy mines!

The mines are the universe. A universe of red and scorched land, shot full of holes, treeless skies and airless air and us flesh-and-bone people toil and sweat amongst it.

All along we thought the mines worked for us, for our families and our futures but it is not the case. The mines are our masters, from Miners to Captains to Adventurers. Yes, we might be powerful and wily, but we are nymphs and piskies by comparison. There are some round here think different, my dear father included, but they are wrong and are foolhardy to think so.

Certain as the sea keeps crashing on the shore, the wheels of industry will keep turning and copper and tin will spew from the earth. We need the mines, like a great buzzard feeding her babies, the mines keep us alive.

The Mines are God and love and life and death! And the Mines are the beginning and the middle and the end!

One by one, like skinny rats, hungry dogs, the men disappear down a dank hole; swallowed whole. And the mines whisper 'You are mine, you are mine, you are mine!'

Matthew strides from the stage.

Bill Scott

Writer, Playwright, Artistic Director of Miracle Theatre, Filmmaker
Constantine

I've got a tiny office, which overlooks the garden. I'm not particularly attached to this space – it's just somewhere to keep my books and stuff.

But I do like the view. There are lots of odd relics from the past in here but the thing I couldn't do without has to be the laptop.

I find that the best thinking happens when I'm propped up in bed. So all initial ideas and early writing are done there. I will only sit at a desk to make a fair copy. My theory is that the brain goes into a more meditative state and hence deeper thinking when the body's relaxed.

I do research at a desk but if I need to resolve a plot then I need to lounge. So my process is to slump in a meditative state, scribbling longhand and then revise on the laptop. However, when working out dialogue I like to walk, especially along the cliff paths, so I can say it out loud.

I keep working until a piece is written and don't have a particular timetable but I absolutely need to have deadlines to work to.

I started writing plays because as a director I wanted to create new work. Initially, I collaborated with Steve Clarke, though it seldom felt like work, just lots of laughter. We took notes during our sessions and then I'd shape it. I've been writing or adapting plays for over thirty-five years. I've also written a wholefood cookbook and beekeeping guide for beginners.

As a procrastinator I will sharpen pencils, tidy and clean, 'research' the Internet, sort files on the laptop. It always feels like a massive task to get started with but is extremely satisfying once I'm off.

Unlovable Me sung by the Monster in 'Frankenstein!'

By Bill Scott with music by Tom Adams (2012)

The sum of my parts is not perfect

They combine to hideous effect

To say I'm a blot on God's landscape

Would be – entirely correct

I may seem athletic

But I'm a job lot

This did the pole vault

This put the shot

I've a brain surgeon's brain

My chin is Dan Dare's

My legs did the Can-Can

At the Folies Bergères

This hand was a lumberjack's

This one was Liszt's

Girls killed for these lips

Now they'll never be kissed

Unlovable me

But my heart's like your heart

It feels and it aches

It longs and it leaps

It burns and it breaks

Unlovable me

Pauline Sheppard

Playwright, Short Story Writer, Poet
St Buryan

What makes a good writing space?
An empty head.
Gardening,
driving, walking,
sitting in a café,
alone
or in a crowd,
the ideas flow.
Items: Always, always, always a notebook and a pencil
(2B)
and these days, Voice Memo on the iPod.
for the inspirational space.

The drafting space:
walking between
pen & pencil
in the garden
and
computer
at the desk.
Uninterrupted.
Peace, light
walled in by books
and the
window
to the garden.
No phone.
Very often
music.

I've written with
Beethoven, Miles Davis,
Peter Maxwell Davies,
birdsong and bee song
and I'm flowing.
The final drafts:
glued to keyboard
and desk
unaware of
all else
except
the end
in sight.

What is special about this place as a writing space?
Being only a step away
from outside.
Knowing its sounds,
the dripping tap,
the wind,
the owls,
blackbirds,
scratching mice.
The rain on tin
the cat flap
rattle
wet paws on my knees
asking for food.
Calm. Peaceful. Cluttered. Mine.

What have you written in here?
11 plays, 9 stage adaptations, 8 screenplays,
2 books, countless stories and poems, 22
notebooks.
Do you always work in here?
Always working
even when I think I'm not.

This is where
the granite is dressed
the stones broken
the words hewn
into shape.

Do any of the objects have a special
significance or reason for being here?
All of them.
Grandma's Aladdin Lamp
memory of writing
in the hissing lamplight
no TV
night sounds beyond the thatch
everything possible.

Anglepoise, Applemac
I love you both.
Piano
to take a break.
On shelves:
Dickens, John Steinbeck,
Katherine Mansfield,
Dennis Potter,
Ken Loach, Jim Allen.
Recordings of the extraordinary lives
of ordinary people... inspirational.

Piles of paper,
can't throw out old versions straight away,
might be better than the new one.

Photos
Postcards
Tapes
Life blood
of stories
to come.

The mornings are mine,
for writing,
in the world of
desk.
Keep away!
Sometimes,
mornings
go on
into night.

Procrastination Activities

Filling in questionnaires, answering emails,
Walking, gardening, driving,
talking
to people
and the cat.
Coffee, Tea,
Glenmorangie,
Guinness.
Piano playing
& Housework.
Anything!
Ed Reardon
on Radio Four.

A Cornish Hedge up Bissoe from the play Hedge by Pauline Sheppard

The voice is Standback's. Standback is a Cornish Hedger, champion arm wrestler, and philosopher. He's called Standback because, well, because he doesn't.

There's a philosophy an' a practicality to a trade like hedging. Like when you're tobbin' off, seeds of the future's in the past, in the earth you throw up top in the autumn. Take time to learn that… There's a right way an' a wrong way, an' everyone have his own way, you got to live it to know.

I like to work alone. Thass what I love. I like to feel the wind on my face, hear the birds, not just the singin'. I like to hear the wings skirring. What other job give you that? Why else do a job like this?… You got to love the country you're workin' with. You got to be a part of it. You got to listen to it… taste it.

It all changed after the war when farmers got on tractors. The old roadman who used to weed round a group of foxgloves an' cut back the corner for the motorist, now he was a gardener. Up in the cab of a four by four tractor with the radio on, a man don't see the butterflies getting torn to death by the flail. Thass because he idden a gardener. He's in his head, worrying about his family, how he'll pay the mortgage… Now, here's the thing, here's the paradox… that man in the cab, he's just the same as the Neolithic man who built hedges in the first place! All he want is to protect his crops and feed his family. He's different but the same, see.

Best time of night, dusk… stones nearly gone quiet, jus' sittin' with the hedge, listenin' to the life in it. Beetle rustlin', or lizard. Used to see lizards all the time. Don't see so many nowadays. This one time, I'd just tobbed off a piece up Bissoe way. One of they quiet and misty evenings when the past come up an' meet you. I was sittin' quiet like, leanin' against the foot of the old hedge, down the field aways from where I'd been working. Up come this fox, sat next to me, so close I could smell his fur, musty like. He'd been around some. He looks at me an' then scratches an' yawns, disdainful like, an' he turns away an' picks a blackberry, real delicate… nose titched up at the end, lip curled back, an' just nipped it off with his front teeth. Nosed in an' around without getting scratched nor tangled like I do with the bramble. "Thass right, boy," I thought. "You enjoy that. Thass yours, that is." They berries were set just right for him, low in the field. Must've been cut well back last year grow like that… cut by hand, the old way. Fresh an' young, whole crop of 'em, real good height for a fox. Must've been five minutes or so, me sittin', that old fox nosin' an' pickin'. Then he juss looks round 'sif to say "I'm off now, pard." An' he's up top the hedge an' gone.

You got to love the country you're workin' with. Thass what I think.

Penelope Shuttle

Poet
Falmouth

I've lived in this house for a long time and have worked in three rooms over that time. I'm now in the attic which used to be my daughter's bedroom. There are views over the Fal Estuary.

I need a window. Natural light is more important than a view, though I love to see the yachts out on the water, and I feel connected to the buzz of the town as I can see Events Square and the Maritime Museum from up here.

I need lots of floor space as I tend to drop notebooks on the floor when working – sometimes the floor is covered in stepping-stones of books and notebooks. I write longhand first-drafts and then I type up the drafts on the computer. There must be no phone or mobile. It is a dedicated space.

I also have a room at my widowed mother's where I work at my father's desk. It is very quiet. I like to write at a desk, not on a sofa with a laptop.

I will often go to cafés to edit. My late husband, the poet Peter Redgrave, and I used to work in tandem and would go out together to cafés to workshop our poems. We did lots of work on The Wise Wound in this fashion, and while on walks around Falmouth.

I'm a morning person, really. I like to start working the earlier the better and I usually stop about 2pm for a late lunch. In the afternoons I will read or see friends or prepare for other work, or go for a walk. I also fit in times for reading work by people I am mentoring, or preparing for workshops.

I collect objects – mainly stones but they are not for inspiration, really, just simple pleasure.

I'm an incubator. I put things away to work on later. I am currently un-incubating, though! I'm going through and rewriting poems I have squirreled away for weeks or months. Everything is dated and filed…if somewhat haphazardly!

I have written all my publications here since 2010 – Sandgrain and Hourglass, 2012, In The Snowy Air: a pamphlet, 2014, and Unsent: New and Selected poems 1980 – 2012.

I'm currently working on new poems.

Down to the water

I go down to the water
to have a shoofty
at the brand-new Bronze Age boat
moored hardby
Salt-limbed
the hand-honed craft weathers
and waits
for its maiden voyage
Three oak trees made it
along with unhurried hands
We saw the builders in the Ship Museum
axe and awl and hemp
making the time-travelling boat
old and new at once
like the sea

D M Thomas

Novelist, Poet, Playwright
Truro

I like to be surrounded by friendly objects. I have photographs of my parents, a portrait of Anna Akhmatova and books, lots of books. Pushkin is said to have waved at his books in his last moments saying 'Farewell my friends'. I like peace, quiet but not silence. There needs to be music, tranquil classical music. I like to look out on something pleasant but not too exuberant. This room is on the first floor and looks over trees, greenery and wild ground. Then I need my computer, notebook, pen and e-cigarette.

I am no Trappist monk but over the years I have been able to create a sense of silence here, a creative atmosphere in which to write. Eventually something comes.

As well as here, I do write on used envelopes, in the car or about the house. Usually when I come to type it up, I can't read my writing.

I don't really relax and always have something on the go.

I've written over half my novels here, from Flying into Love, the biography of Solzhenitsyn, collections of poems, a translation of Pushkin's Onegin, to Hell Fire Cornwall, a play about rugby.

Until 2000 I wrote mostly prose but it is a huge physical effort to write a novel, so for the last ten years I have returned to poetry.

I do like a sense of routine. I won't begin writing till after coffee at about eleven where I begin by looking at work from the night before, gathering scraps. Then there's lunch. I write again in the afternoon till about four, maybe take a nap. Then it is wine at six. This is very important as ideas that I may have missed when concentrating, take shape when in a more swimming state. In the evening I relax with TV or reading but then may go back to my study before bed. If I haven't written anything half decent that day I don't feel good.

With poetry I like to write longhand first as each word and syllable is important. I like the weight of the pen in this process. Whereas, with prose I go straight to the computer as it is not so exacting.

I do have a vague sense of where I am going with a novel; I will have plotted the first couple of chapters but from there on it is a voyage of discovery; as Robert Frost said, 'No surprise for the writer, no surprise for the reader'.

I am not a procrastinator in any way, in fact I militate against it ,I am an obsessive. I drive myself with the feeling that I must get on.

Centenary Thanksgiving for Thomas Merritt by D M Thomas

'Order of Service: Please stand as the Dean conducts the Deputy Lieutenant…
to her seat at the front of the nave…' (Truro Cathedral, June 2008).

'Do 'ee mind if I sit here a minute, my 'andsome?'
I was on a bench, smoking, before the walk home.
He sat; the crowd was still streaming out
and past us, silent, sober, in the mild evening light.
He pointed to the Order of Service in my lap:
'I still haven't got over the first shock. Stand up!

– stand up for they! I'd have turned in my grave
 if I'd been in it; when they wafted up the nave
it was like they was puttin' we simple folk in our place,
tampin' down the mood and the spirit, in case
"Hark the glad sound!" sparked off an explosion
of full-voiced, rapturous, Cornish emotion.

Like Billy Bray, I never stood up for anyone;
and do'ee know why? – because I am a King's son!
Worship, for we, was like the blasting of rocks
in the bal, not that row of pasty-faced men in frocks
who kept us flat, like a drizzle on Carn Brea,
by getting up and bleating in turn, with nothin' to say.

They'd 'a' been throwed from the pulpit home Redruth
– or more likely, chucked off the cliff at Hell's Mouth.
And where was the thunder of triumphant Calvary
in the Bible readings? Wisht as gnats' wee,
it hurt me to hear it! Somebody must have sieved
all the glory out, like they wanted to say He never lived –

the Infant Stranger, Jesse's tender rod! I tell 'ee, boy,
it felt like a museum; with less joy
than there was in my hovel with sand on the floor
when I called for a pen to write down one more
heavenly tune before I went – one more Hosanna!
And I've heard my curls from Moonta to Montana

sung with ecstasy by crowds of Cousin Jacks,
deep underground, or in chapels no more'n shacks,
but as to that gilded prison there, I thirst
for the hour when "the gates of brass before Him burst,
The iron fetters yield!" Well, see 'ee 'gain,
my lover.' He shuffled off down St. Mary's Lane,

warbling, in both contralto and baritone,
"The glorious Lord,

Of Life comes down!"… a crazy tramp who grieved
for majestic words, and preachers who believed,
and thought he was poor Tom, down a mine at eleven,
his body clamped by pain, his head in heaven.

Thomas Merritt (1863-1908), frail, self-taught musician and composer of famous Christmas carols. Billy Bray (1794-1868), miner and inspirational preacher. 'Bal' – mine; 'wisht' – weak; 'curls' – carols.

Elaine Ruth White

Playwright and Librettist
Helston

I was an Army 'brat', and as a family we were constantly on the move, from one set of Married Quarters to the next, one county to the next, one country to the next. Cornwall gave me my first ever sense of 'place' as 'home'. Because I never lived in one house for more than two years – and every move meant a clear out – anything excess to requirements was ditched, regardless of emotional attachment! Thinking about it, I never lived in one house longer than three years until I was 36! Maybe that's why my writing space has become so focussed inside my head.

Perhaps growing up with an Army background also explains why I don't tend to collect objects to inspire me. All those years of moving house meant all those years of packing and unpacking! Traveling light, in all things, has become a way of life.

One of the reasons we moved to this house was so I could have my own office – my own private space to write. But we've only been here a few months and, at the moment, I'm putting things onto paper in the dining room where I feel most comfortable. I like this space as it's free flowing, warm and light, and linked to the outside. I can get up and walk around when I need to; I hate to feel shut in or trapped. Upstairs I have my own room, my space to write, but it feels more enclosed.

For someone who writes so much in her head, I buy lots of notebooks, dozens of them, with brightly coloured covers. I love writing on the first few pristine pages, but then go back to the old habit of writing in my head. Committing to print comes quite late in the process and then straight onto laptop.

Deadlines dictate discipline, of course, but I'm not someone who begins writing at nine, or commits to a thousand words a day. I like to write a clean first draft and then become very focussed when it comes to cutting or editing.

How do I procrastinate? I like gaming, particularly games that set up new worlds with new characters. It's very escapist. As I am fairly obsessed with text, gaming is a great way of relaxing as it's so visual. Sadly I never procrastinate by doing something useful like housework or ironing!

I started out as a non-fiction writer and had several books published before exploring creative writing by way of poetry. I love writing for theatre and opera and hearing my words sung is one of my greatest joys.

After this interview, Elaine moved into her new writing room.

From The Serpentine Turner by Elaine Ruth White

TOM: Speak stone to me.

JEM: Speak?

TOM: Tell me about the stone.

JEM: Stone. Right … stone. Well, basically... the stone...

TOM: Let me speak stone to you. What do you see?

JEM: It's round.

TOM: It isn't round. Look at the markings.

JEM: Like a snake's skin.

TOM: What else?

JEM: It's the colour of dried blood.

TOM: Look harder.

JEM: Oh yeah. Breasts.

TOM: Breasts?

JEM: There.

TOM: Breasts, my… that's life… captured as it was a million years ago. When I look at this stone, I see the world as it used to be – honest, genuine, free. I look at the ground and see the land fresh each day. That's how I always want to see it, so it startles me, catches me by surprise. You can trust the land.

JEM: How come some of it's red and some's green?

TOM: More to the point, how come some of it was about to go missing?

YOUNG WRITERS

Kernow Education Arts Partnership (KEAP)'s business has always been arts in education in schools in Cornwall. In 2013 we launched a new venture called The Story Republic which has a focus on supporting creative writing and literacy in schools and community groups through the arts. This has been an extraordinary journey of discovery, working with writers and artists, creating a performance team called The Story Republicans who have been animating feasts and festivals with their original blend of spoken word and song and most recently partnering with Discover in Stratford to host an installation inspired by children's writer Oliver Jeffers.

But core to all this work is developing talent and giving children and young people the chance to disappear into their imaginations and grow through the power of their stories and inventions. The Story Republic has been doing this through writers working in partnership with teachers to encourage new writing which is displayed in the physical Story Republic and online. But we have also begun to think how and where children write in school, how they can learn from professional writers and how we can encourage independence in writing. And so began the pilot project A Space to Write in three schools in Cornwall. Wyl Menmuir has written an account of that project.

We are also featuring Kernow Young Writers which has been set up by KEAP and Annamaria Murphy to encourage enthusiastic and talented writers aged from 13-19. They choose to come to this group because they are in a space with likeminded people who are passionate about reading and writing and for whom it is cool to want to be scribbling in a notebook all day. For them it is more about time and people than the physical space.

Encouraging the next generation of writers

Writing is, without doubt, one of the most difficult things we're required to learn as children. And it's perhaps a sign of its complexity that it never really seems to get any easier the older we get. While the challenges themselves may change, the level of challenge doesn't.

To complicate things further, my experience as a writer and teacher suggests the way writing - composition in particular - is taught and practised in schools can be at odds with the way professional writers really write.

We know successful composition involves time, experience and reflection. But how often are these elements played out in the classroom? And is it surprising that many children choose not to write, except when required to by their teacher?

This is where Space to Write comes in. Over the past year, working with KEAP, The Learning Institute and schools in Cornwall, I've been exploring the role of space in developing children's independent writing. We worked with the schools to carve out time and space for children to develop as writers in their own right, to develop positive attitudes towards writing, and the motivation to write independently.

The spaces they developed differed hugely, from huts in playgrounds to tipis in the woods, from a hidden writing hideaway to a pop up in the library. We explored the idea of writing space in a whole range of ways too, not just the physical spaces, but exploring the time set aside for children's independent writing, giving children their own private writing books and affording them a much greater degree of freedom and autonomy than they might otherwise have been given.

And what we found (though the project was only small and we're looking to explore the area in much more depth) indicated children's independence and autonomy does have an impact on their motivation to write. We saw children using their independent writing time to concentrate on vastly differing aspects of writing. Some children worked on developing their writing stamina, developing longer and more complex narratives, while others experimented with a range of different forms, and others still concentrated on their handwriting and presentation. And that choice to concentrate appeared to be both liberating and motivating, leading the children to engage with their own writing in new ways.

What we saw in the schools suggests to me that providing space for writing that is not constantly monitored and assessed may help to free up children to develop as writers. It's not to say the explicit teaching of writing skills – grammar, spelling, punctuation, rhetoric, developing a coherent argument and so on – aren't vital. Or that children shouldn't be assessed. What it does suggest is that teachers and children have much to learn from the methods, habits, processes and spaces of working writers and authors and that exploring the complexities and subtleties of writing may have real implications for how we provide our children with the best experiences, the ones that turn them into lifelong writers.

And aside from anything else, the Space to Write project opened up valuable dialogues between teachers and children. Authentic dialogues in which children and adults explored writing and writing processes together. After all, if it's true that writing doesn't get easier the older and more experienced we get, we're all in the same boat really.

'You can explore your ability to write whatever you want, without being criticised.' Year 5 child

'The space is symbolic as well as literal.' Teacher

Although we have not included the many inspirational and influential writers who have lived and worked in Cornwall but are not longer with us, A Space to Write would not be complete for KEAP, without acknowledging artist, playwright, lobster fisherman and much missed friend Nick Darke

Many writers included in here knew Nick personally, most, if not all will know of or have seen his work and we are very grateful to Jane Darke for allowing us to use this next passage to bring the book to a close.

Perhaps, when you next see a lobster fisherman hauling up a pot, you might see the process a little differently...

Nick Darke

Nick was a playwright, screen writer and environmental campaigner. He lived where he was born in the parish of St. Eval on the North Cornish coast. His plays have been produced by, amongst others, The National Theatre, The Royal Shakespeare Company, Kneehigh, The Royal Court, BBC Radio and Television, notably The King of Prussia, The Riot, The Dead Monkey and The Body. He was a Bard of the Gorseth Kernow.

We are especially grateful to Jane Darke for allowing us to use his wonderful words in this book.

On the face of it there's nothing to compare lobster fishing with playwriting but delve down and the similarities are there. Both are solitary activities, meticulously prepared then thrown to the whim of uncontrollable forces such as the Atlantic Ocean or theatre directors. One plunders humanity's detritus, the other baits with putrid meat. Both, when successful, are ludicrously over-paid and their practitioners wonder where the next one's coming from.

So how does lobster fishing meld with playwriting? Do they integrate on a day-to-day basis? Here's routine one. Wake up at dawn. Spend five minutes watching sea through bedroom window. There's a swell fetching in and breaking onto the shore but it's not too big to launch. Switch on computer, go outside and check weather. Wind force and direction are critical. Haul on 'skins (oil). Return to screen and click on current play. Sit at desk in fishing gear and read yesterday's work, taking care not to drop particles of sand and dried bait into keyboard. Absorb play whilst thinking of fish. (Zen moment) Launch boat. Haul, clear, bait and shoot pots. Talk to self. Discuss catch so far. Study swell condition round Turtle Rock and debate safety margin for far pot. Push thoughts of play to back of mind and head for Turtle. Swell is big. Realisation. Wind strength underestimated. Play forgotten. Reach pot. Engine neutral. Haul in slack rope. Gigantic swell. Engine falters. Fuck. Raise throttle one notch. Engine screams. Sea in turmoil round rock. Haul pot. Wind carries boat directly towards rock. Pot reaches gunwhale as boat nudges rock. Massive lobster. Wind drops, swells shrink, engine purrs. Offer short prayer to Poseidon. Clear pot, bait it, re-shoot. Steam home rehearsing Oscar acceptance speech, playwright and lobster fisherman in perfect harmony. Remove 'skins. Write play. Routine two. Wake up, check sea. Too big. No fishing. Think of play. Sleep.

Seizure of moment is the key skill that a lobster fisherman shares with the playwright. Playwriting involves accumulating diverse gobbets then judging the perfect time to feed them into the computer. Start to write too early with too few gobbets and you dry up, frustrated. If you leave it too late the material grows stale and the process becomes laboured. It's the same with lobsters. You shoot your pot, you leave it lie. The prey smells the bait, expresses interest, wanders over and takes a look with those stalky eyes. It crawls around the pot and probes for the bait but can't quite reach, so it swims in through the neck, dines and enters the parlour. Trapped. If you haul your pot too early you've lost your fish but if you leave it too late and the sea gets up, the pot shifts and in two days it's gone.

The playwright who is also a lobster fisherman works to a lobster fisherman's time frame. Life is governed by the moon. Writing becomes tidal, low water the deadline. In winter the boat is seldom launched due to adverse sea conditions. Fishing is reduced to a single pot attached to a ring bolt on an island, and the journey there includes a wade through bollock crushing cold water. On rare occasions it is possible to launch at Christmas when there's a high pressure sitting on us and the sea goes flat as a pea on a plate. The sun shines. The air is crisp. If the tide is neapish (not too high or too low) the playwright takes his boat and shoots a net across Trescore.

This is a magic, tranquil time. A moment stolen from the elements. He shouldn't be out there. Poseidon has blinked. The playwright hauls the net and alters his diet to bass, dover sole, turbot. He beaches the boat. There are no people about. No dogs. The second-home-owners are tucked away in House One, Surbiton. He lies back on the crust of frosted sand, closes his eyes and dreams. The playwright becomes not lobster fisherman, but lobster. The lobster occupies a hole in the rock and emerges at night. It is a solitary, cautious beast with few predators. Fiercely combative when threatened, it has survived millions of years without a brain. All actions are programmed, instinctive, patterned, like a play. Plays are blueprints for three dimensions. The playwright's tools are language, actors, action, his habitat the stage, the black hole…he's woken from his reverie by the sound of a shorebreak. He surveys the sea. Dolphins swim around Turtle Rock amongst a growing thunderswell which ten minutes ago wasn't there. Gannets dive. Guillemots and razorbills bob and duck and disappear into the troughs between Atlantic rollers. The sea, once more, is an alien place. Back to computer. Write play.

WRITER BIOGRAPHIES

Bert Biscoe

Bert Biscoe was brought up in Stithians. His father was a GP and his mother a nurse. He attended Truro School and later Bangor University. Bert has had an extensive career in Cornwall's creative industry as a musician, writer, administrator, manager, event coordinator and animateur. Today he lives in Truro and is a cabinet member within Cornwall Council. www.bertbiscoe.co.uk

Megan Chapman

MCMC – aka Megan Chapman is a critically acclaimed performance word artist. Inspired by the rap music of Eminem at the tender age of fifteen and using the media of poetry, rap, freestyle and spoken word, MCMC uses her diverse skills and interests to communicate views and visions of the world both as she sees it and through the eyes of others. She writes to connect herself to people and them to each other, giving the unheard a collective voice to be shouted out on stage. www.mcmcspoken.co.uk

Jon Cleave

Jon is probably best known as front man and bass singer of over twenty years with the Cornish sea shanty group The Fisherman's Friends, for whom he has evolved as a lyricist, arranger and composer. He has toured extensively and made numerous TV and radio appearances. Jon has performed live at many leading venues, most notably on the Pyramid Stage at Glastonbury and in front of fifty thousand people at the Proms in the Park in 2014. He has an acting credit to his name for his lead role in the short film 'Black Car Home'. Jon is the author and illustrator of the popular series of seven children's books about Gully, the mischievous and wicked Cornish seagull. 2014 saw the publication of his first 'grown up' novel, Nasty Pasty, for which in 2015 he was the proud recipient of the Holyer an Gof Prize for best Cornish novel. www.thegullery.co.uk

Jane Darke

Jane Darke is a 'cliff dwelling scavenger who happens to live in Cornwall'. Her influences are many and varied. She works as a painter, writer and film maker. Each discipline has heroes: Picasso, Richard Long, Khalo, O'Keeffe, Bruce Chatwin, Virginia Woolf, Defoe, Dylan, Björk, Mallick, Kubrick, Heaney and of course her late husband Nick Darke. Her memoir Held by the Sea about love and landscape was published by Souvenir Press in 2011. Nick dies at the beginning of the book but it's surprisingly funny. Humour is important in everything. In the last year Jane has been working on a documentary about Charles Causley, to be finished this autumn. She is working on a children's book with publisher Mabecron books and her film The Wrecking Season was shown at The Maritime Museum, Falmouth, and on PBS America.

www.janedarke.co.uk www.nickdarke.net www.thewreckingseason.com www.theartofcatchinglobsters.com

Bob Devereux

Bob Devereux has been an active member of the arts community in St Ives, Cornwall since the late 1960s. He ran The Salthouse Gallery in St Ives for thirty years, from 1980 to 2010, representing many contemporary artists and staging eighty-one shows a year. As an artist he has exhibited widely in Britain and abroad.

As a poet he has collaborated with 11 composers and provided libretti for eight operas which have been performed in Germany and Japan. His poems have been carved in oak and cut in granite. One piece, Morris Room, was chosen by Billy Connolly as one of his Desert Island Discs. With Martin Val Baker he resurrected The St Ives September Festival, in 1993, which still runs every year, and he is Director of the St Ives Literature Festival, held annually in May. He is also responsible for a weekly event for poets, storytellers and songwriters which is staged on Thursdays at the St Ives Arts Club.

Mac Dunlop

Mac founded The Poetry Point in 2007 – intended as a website portal to poetry and spoken word events and information in Cornwall and the South West. Since then, along with the artist and academic Dr. Annie Lovejoy, he's hosted the weekly Caravanserai Fireside Sessions of spoken word and music which take place every summer on the Roseland Peninsula.

Mac also works as a radio producer, recently developing scripts collaboratively in the community, and with Hall For Cornwall. He also publishes as the Pluto Press Award winning cartoonist MacD. His latest collection of cartoons and writing, "The Enigma Deviations", is available online through the satirical website Politoons. bespokenwords@yahoo.com

Patrick Gale

Patrick was born on 31 January 1962 on the Isle of Wight. He was the youngest of four – one sister, two brothers, spread over ten years. The family moved to London, where his father ran Wandsworth Prison, then to Winchester. At eight Patrick began boarding as a Winchester College Quirister at the cathedral choir school, Pilgrims'. At thirteen he went on to Winchester College. He finished his formal education with an English degree from New College, Oxford in 1983.

He has never had a grown-up job. For three years he lived at a succession of addresses, from a Notting Hill bedsit to a crumbling French chateau. While working on his first novels he eked out his slender income with odd jobs: as a typist, a singing waiter, a designer's secretary, a ghost-writer for an encyclopedia of the musical and, increasingly, as a book reviewer.

His first two novels, The Aerodynamics of Pork and Ease were published by Abacus on the same day in June 1986. The following year he moved to Camelford near the north coast of Cornwall and began a love affair with the county that has fed his work ever since. He now lives in the far west, on a farm near Land's End with his husband, Aidan Hicks. There they raise beef cattle and grow barley. As well as writing and an obsessive passion for gardening, Patrick chairs the North Cornwall Book Festival, is a patron of Penzance LitFest and a director of both Endelienta and The Charles Causley Trust. His chief extravagance in life is opera tickets.

Rebecca Gregson

Journalist turned novelist, Rebecca Gregson wrote her first winning words as a ten-year-old girl, holed up in a wet Cornish cottage on holiday with her Dad and his new wife, who had hairy armpits and definitely preferred dogs to children. Her indignant short story went on to win a school competition – the only prize she has ever won, as it turns out.

Growing up in a thatched 16th century village pub in Somerset, Rebecca attributes her ear for dialogue and her instinct for a story to her habit of eavesdropping on bar talk from the bottom stone step of a forgotten staircase the other side of a locked door.

A postgraduate journalism course led her to newspapers and radio, joining BBC Radio Cornwall as a reporter and presenter where listeners knew her as Rebecca Pickford.

She swapped fact for fiction as a means of juggling work and a young family. With six novels now published, she is toying with the idea of forgiving the hairy armpit woman. It's either that, or writing her into the TV script she's currently working on.

Carl Grose

Carl Grose was born and raised in Truro, Cornwall. His plays include Grand Guignol, Superstition Mountain, 49 Donkeys Hanged, The 13 Midnight Challenges of Angelus Diablo, Gargantua and Horse Piss For Blood. Over the past twenty years he has worked with the internationally acclaimed Kneehigh Theatre as both actor and writer. Writing for Kneehigh includes Tristan & Yseult, The Bacchae, Blast!, Cymbeline, Hansel & Gretel, The Wild Bride and, most recently, Dead Dog In A Suitcase (and other love songs) – a new version of The Beggar's Opera. Carl has also written for Spymonkey, National Theatre of Wales, Told By An Idiot, and BBC TV and Radio. Carl is currently writing new plays for the RSC, The National, and The Drum Theatre, Plymouth.

Alyson Hallett

Alyson Hallett's latest book of poems is On Ridgegrove Hill (Atlantic Press, 2015). This book was made in collaboration with designer Phyllida Bluemel, and is a result of the residency at Cyprus Well. Alyson is a prize-winning poet whose work has been broadcast on Radio 4, carved into a pavement in the city of Bath and etched into stained glass windows. For the past fifteen years she has curated the ongoing poetry/public art project, The Migration Habits of Stones. For more information please visit www.thestonelibrary.com

Seth Hampshire

Seth Hampshire describes himself as a beat poet. When he was at university he quietly started writing poetry, but always and only for himself. For one of his projects, he was meant to hand in a book of images with text but instead handed in a book and CD. The CD was the first ever recording of his work. He expected to fail the assignment but ended up with top marks; this was the beginning of his career as a beat poet. A few years later Seth was introduced to Chris Hines who started Surfers Against Sewage and Chris offered him his first gig at Global Cornwall in 2011. In the last few years Seth has been working with Annamaria Murphy as part of the Kneehigh Theatre Connections project. He was part of The Story Republic talent development programme and has worked with a number of youth organisations, including Carefree Cornwall.

Amanda Harris

Amanda Harris is director of KEAP. She has a passion for arts in education, in particular encouraging creative writing and a love of stories and literature. She is the founder of The Story Republic with Annamaria Murphy and Helen Reynolds which in itself has grown out of many years of collaboration on projects such as Kneehigh's Shop of Stories and Wild Walks, Scavel an Gow, a writers' collective, and many artist led immersive spaces. She does have a shed which her husband built her in the garden but it has currently been subsumed as an extra bedroom. But in its peace and spartan atmosphere she has written a lot of short stories, a novel and a stack of funding applications.

Pol Hodge

Pol Hodge passed the highest Cornish language examination with distinction and was made a Bardh an Yeth of Gorsedh Kernow in 1991 at An Garrek / Roche, taking the bardic name Mab Stenek Veur.

He has written two solo volumes of poetry, Mowth On Un Like Dolcoath Shaft and 'Otter Than A Bitch Mackerel. Pol Hodge has been featured in many anthologies and performed in Kernewek at over 350 performances throughout Cornwall and in Scotland, Ireland, the Isle of Man, Wales, Brittany, England and America. "Hodge is the real deal, his poetry is created in Kernewek – it is not translation. He then really makes it come alive by performing at Dew Vardh concerts." – Victor Hendra.

Mark Jenkin

Mark is a screenwriter and filmmaker based in Newlyn, West Cornwall. He is currently in pre-production with his new film Flowtide, working with producers Kate Byers and Linn Waite at Early Day Films. He is also writing a biopic of St. Ives artist Alfred Wallis, having been the recipient of The Nick Darke Award for Writing in October 2014.

He is an associate lecturer in Film and Moving Image at Falmouth University and is the author of the SLDG13 Film Manifesto which promotes the aesthetic and practical benefits of handmade celluloid work. His studio is within the Newlyn School of Art and as a member of the prestigious Newlyn Society of Artists his short-form work has been exhibited in galleries in the UK and on mainland Europe.

Mercedes Kemp

Mercedes Kemp was born and grew up in Andalucia, Southern Spain. For the past forty years she has lived in West Cornwall. As a member of WildWorks Core Artistic Team she works developing storylines and text. Her role also involves creating and maintaining relationships with host communities, exploring their relationships with place and memory and adapting text to fit each new location. Her freelance work includes commissions for The Eden Project, The Guardian and BBC Radio 3. She worked as a writer for Kneehigh Theatre in Strange Cargo, Manel's Mango, Shop of Stories, Doubtful Island, Island of Dreams and A Very Old Man with Enormous Wings. She is a founding member of the writing and performing collective Scavel an Gow. Mercedes is Senior Lecturer in Fine Art at University College Falmouth.

Liz Kessler

Liz Kessler has written sixteen novels for children and young adults. Her books have sold over four million copies worldwide, have appeared on the New York Times Bestsellers list and have been translated into twenty-five languages. Liz writes for all ages from early readers to older teens. Her younger books feature a pirate dog based on her own Dalmatian, Poppy. Her middle grade books include mermaids, fairies, superpowers and time travel, and her first Young Adult novel, Read Me Like A Book, published in May 2015, features a seventeen-year-old girl coming out and has been described by international bestselling author Jodi Picoult as 'a welcome reminder that love is love, no matter what,' and by bestselling author Sarah Waters as 'a warm, funny, engaging novel about friendship, family and following your heart.' www.lizkessler.co.uk

Emma Mansfield

Emma Mansfield cut her teeth in the film and broadcast industry as a researcher and production coordinator. In 2002 she moved to Cornwall to work with the arts and interpretation team at the Eden Project. In 2006 Emma became Eden's first Creative Producer and headed up 'Site Wide Live', a 15 strong department of staff and freelancers responsible for delivering the onsite visitor experience, touring projects and The Eden Sessions. In her spare time Emma is a yoga teacher, choir leader and runs a small publishing company Lovely Little Books.

Philip Marsden

Philip Marsden is the award-winning author of a number of books of travel, history and fiction. He spent the 1990s travelling to and writing about the Middle East and the territories of the old Soviet Union, years which produced books like The Crossing Place: A Journey among the Armenians, The Bronski House and The Spirit-Wrestlers. His more recent books – The Levelling Sea (2011) and Rising Ground (2014) – concern aspects of British landscape and place. He is a fellow of the Royal Society of Literature and his work has been translated into fifteen languages. He now lives in Cornwall on the tidal reaches of the Upper Fal with his family and a number of boats.

Wyl Menmuir

Wyl writes about life on the fringes. Born in Stockport in 1979, he now lives on the north coast of Cornwall, where he explores the narrative truths of the unsettled and the unsettling. He believes in fiction that draws on the deeply personal and the deeply weird.

As well as writing fiction, Wyl is a freelance editor and literacy consultant. When he's not writing, you'll find him out on the water or up on the cliffs – anywhere there's a view of the sea. His debut novel, The Many, is due to be published by Salt in 2016.

wylmenmuir.co.uk

Callum Mitchell

Callum is a writer, theatre-maker, producer and performer from Newlyn, Cornwall.

He is founder and joint artistic director of DIY theatre company, Silly Boys, alongside musician Seamas Carey. He regularly performs at festivals across the UK and delivers workshops to children and adults in creative writing and poetry. He also works in film. He is currently writing a new show about the village where he is from, as well as curating a mixed-media exhibition to accompany its debut at Newlyn Arts festival 2015. The show is entitled Always Changing, Forever The Same.

Graham Mitchell

Graham Mitchell was brought up in the Redruth area; his father was a singer and his uncle was a writer so music and performance and the making of both were the backdrop to his young life.

At 18 he couldn't wait to get away from Cornwall – the usual thing of too much small-town life. Instead of going to drama school he managed to blag his way into various theatre companies and Theatre in Education companies in London and Yorkshire. Very soon opportunities arose to co-devise and eventually to write for actors and performers.

Television came along later. Graham quickly fell in love with the collaborative nature of working in that medium (and still is). His scripts are the very beginning of the process and then everything stems from that.

Annamaria Murphy

Annamaria Murphy was born in Polperro and spent most of her childhood staring at boats and hiding under tables listening to grown-ups. Founder member of "The Witchy Eye Club", aged eight till eleven. In 1970 her English teacher, Mr Taffy Owens gave her a copy of "Under Milk Wood", which rocked her world, opening her up to a whole new range of possibilities of words. From that day on she became a secret writer. Then, in 1989 she was asked to play a wild dog in one of Kneehigh's WildWalks but didn't quite cut it as a canine character… so instead she wrote herself the part of Beryl, a shopper lost in the woods.

That was the beginning of her writing career. Today Annamaria writes for Kneehigh Theatre, Cscape Dance, Rogue Theatre, Theatre Alibi, Platform 4, BBC Radio Four and is Artist Director of The Story Republic. When she's not out in her wooden writing shed, she's out in a wooden rowing boat with the Pendeen Gig Club.

Simon Parker

Simon Parker is a playwright, publisher, journalist and bard of Gorsedh Kernow. His plays (Third Light, Gonamena, Mad Dog, The Illegible Bachelor, Seven Stars, Piran) have been staged at Plymouth Barbican Theatre, Sterts Theatre and Plymouth Theatre Royal, as well as touring numerous smaller venues. A founder member of writers' collective Scavel An Gow, his published work includes Solid, Beast, Full As An Egg, Chasing Tales and Horses Stood Still. He has written for Kneehigh, WildWorks and BBC Radio 4 and has won a number of literary and publishing awards, including the Henry Jenner Cup, Sybil Pomeroy Cup, Rosemergy Cup, Holyer An Gof, and Winston Graham Historical Fiction Prize bursary. He runs Scryfa, a publishing company celebrating contemporary Cornish writing. His work as a journalist for the Western Morning News spans nearly thirty years, specialising in Cornish news and issues, and writing and editing the Living Cornwall and Westcountry Life sections. He has three amazing children and lives at Linkinhorne with his lovely missus Jan.

Jane Pugh

During the late 80s Jane worked at a film workshop in Oxford and made documentaries for Channel 4 and film projects that promoted community cohesion. Jane won a place at the National Film and Television School: concentrating on drama, she went on to make 23 short films which won a total of seven prizes, including an Oscar. She worked in drama development for the BBC and script edited on long running drama series. Jane moved to Cornwall in 2000 and began writing her own material, teaching, script editing and project managing. She has worked across all art forms and project managed Morvah Schoolhouse, Carn to Cove and Feast. She is currently lecturing in screenwriting and narrative structure at Falmouth University, finishing her screenplay, working on a site-specific performance project based in Porthleven with a brilliant team of artists, writing and performing short stories and working with exciting, established writers as a script editor.

jane@highstreetcornwall.fsnet.co.uk

Bill Scott

Bill is the founder and Artistic Director of Miracle Theatre, the small-scale touring company based at Krowji in Redruth. Since 1979 the company has produced over 30 open-air summer shows and 15 indoor shows that have toured to community venues across the Southwest. Bill has written or adapted most of these.

He recently wrote the St Austell community play, "As Well Be Shot As Be Starved", about the bread riots in the town in 1847. He has also written and directed six short films and one full-length feature, Tin.

He is the author of the 1970's classic wholefood cookbook 'Food for Thought' and 'Backyard Beekeeping'.

Pauline Sheppard

Pauline Sheppard has lived and worked in Cornwall since 1969. A writer of plays and short stories she writes about the extraordinary qualities of everyday life. Her play Dressing Granite was nominated for the Meyer-Whitworth Award in 1997. She adapted The Ordinalia (The Cornish Mystery Cycle) for the community of St. Just (2000 – 2004).

She is also a performer, founder member of Cornwall Theatre Company (Acorn Theatre) and a bard of the Cornish Gorsedh. Tin & Fishes, her play for voices, has been a set text for Penwith College Media Diploma Course, and is widely used at conferences to illustrate social issues in Cornwall. An extract was published in Planet (The Welsh Internationalist) as part of their 2015 Global Mining feature. Her plays Hevva Hevva and Voyage of The Mystery, written for National Maritime Museum have introduced hundreds of schoolchildren to Cornish history. She has also written for radio and screen but is happiest in theatres.

When she is not writing she loves to sit in her garden. Pauline writes for theatre and screen and has written seven books.

For a full list of plays and publications visit www.paulinesheppard.com

Penelope Shuttle

Penelope Shuttle was born in 1947 in Middlesex, and has lived in Falmouth, Cornwall since 1970, a place which often inspires her current work.

Her husband, Peter Redgrove, died in 2003, and her poetry collection, Redgrove's Wife (2006), is a book of lament and celebration about his life and death, and the loss of her father. It was shortlisted for the 2007 T. S. Eliot Prize and the Forward Poetry Prize (Best Poetry Collection of the Year).

She is also the author of five earlier novels, including All the Usual Hours of Sleeping (1969) and The Mirror of the Giant (1980). With her husband, she published two non-fiction books: The Wise Wound: Eve's Curse and Everywoman (1978), dealing with the psychology and creative aspect of menstruation and its part in redefining the role of women, and its sequel, Alchemy for Women: Personal Transformation Through Dreams and the Female Cycle (1995).

Penelope Shuttle received a Cholmondeley Award in 2007. She reads her poetry throughout the UK and is an experienced poetry tutor. Her latest book is a further collection of poetry, Sandgrain and Hourglass (2010).

Steve Tanner

Since inheriting his uncles Kodak Instamatic at the age of 14 Steve has been addicted to photography. He has exhibited work nationally originating from projects in Northern Ireland, Berlin, China, America, Russia and Japan. Steve has been working commercially for the last 25 years, based in the South West he specialises in working with the counties leading artists, galleries, theatre and dance companies. He says he's not a landscape photographer - hasn't got the patience. He thrives on the challenge of capturing serendipity.

D M Thomas

D M Thomas is a poet and novelist, born in Redruth in 1935, from a mining family. He was educated in Redruth, Melbourne, then New College, Oxford, where he received a First in English. He became a teacher and lecturer, before deciding to write full-time. He has received a Cholmondeley Award for poetry, the Orwell prize for his biography of Alexander Solzhenitsyn, and his bestselling, Booker-nominated third novel (1981) The White Hotel is considered a modern classic, published in over thirty languages. His play Hell Fire Corner was produced at the Hall For Cornwall in 2004. He lives in Truro with his fourth wife Angela, and has three grown-up children.

www.dmthomasonline.net

Elaine Ruth White

Elaine Ruth White has written for page, stage and radio. She was the writer on the award-winning community opera 'One Day, Two Dawns'. Her latest play, The Serpentine Turner, is under consideration for the Bruntwood Prize 2015. www.whitewonders.wix.com/words-like-music Email: white_wonders@btinternet.com

Enormous thanks to

All the writers and their families for giving us access to their private writing spaces and sharing their writing with us. Jane Darke and Tim Neale for allowing us to use photographs and an extract from Nick's work. All the funders who had faith in us to invest in this book, in particular The Arts Council England, Esmée Fairbairn Foundation, RIO and the Challenge Fund, Feast, and the Q fund. Also Ian Bridgenorth, Stephanie Clemens, Helen Reynolds, Felicity Bestwick, Jemima Taylor, Ian Kingsnorth, Paul Colledge, Hall For Cornwall, Ivor & Dan Corbett, Tormark Books, Waterstones Truro, the North Cornwall Book Festival, Rupert Loydell, Neil Scott, Rose Barnecut, Vicky Reece Romain & Charlotte Bone for sound advice and support. All members of the KEAP board.

Debbie Lambert and the children at Tintagel Primary School, Kathy Rowe and the children at Marlborough Primary School, Nathalie Thomas and the students at Richard Lander School, Wyl Menmuir, Nick Appleby and Laura Osborne at The Learning Institute for their commitment and creativity with the education pilot of A Space to Write.